Assessing Critical Thinking in Middle and High Schools

Meeting the Common Core

Rebecca Stobaugh

This book is dedicated to my children.
May they always challenge themselves to reach their full potential.

EYE ON EDUCATION
6 DEPOT WAY WEST, SUITE 106
LARCHMONT, NY 10538
(914) 833–0551
(914) 833–0761 fax
www.eyeoneducation.com

Library of Congress Cataloging-in-Publication Data

Stobaugh, Rebecca.
   Assessing critical thinking in middle and high schools: meeting the
common core / Rebecca Stobaugh.
        pages cm
 Includes bibliographical references.
 ISBN 978-1-59667-233-8
1. Thought and thinking--Study and teaching (Middle school)
2. Thought and thinking--Study and teaching (High School) 3. Critical
thinking--Study and teaching (Middle School) 4. Critical thinking--
Study and teaching (Secondary) I. Title.
 LB1590.3.S496 2013
 370.15′2--dc23   2012037714

Sponsoring Editor: Robert Sickles
Copyeditor: Laurie Lieb
Designer and Compositor: Rick Soldin
Cover Designer: Dave Strauss, 3FoldDesign

Also Available from Eye On Education

Assessing Critical Thinking in Elementary Schools:
Meeting the Common Core
Rebecca Stobaugh

Rigor Is NOT a Four- Letter Word
Barbara R. Blackburn

Critical Thinking and Formative Assessments
Increasing the Rigor in Your Classroom
Betsy Moore and Todd Stanley

Rigor Made Easy: Getting Started
Barbara R. Blackburn

Rigor in Your School
A Toolkit for Leaders
Ronald Williamson and Barbara R. Blackburn

Rigorous Schools and Classrooms
Leading the Way
Ronald Williamson and Barbara R. Blackburn

Teacher-Made Assessments
How to Connect Curriculum, Instruction, and Student Learning
Christopher R. Gareis and Leslie W. Grant

Differentiated Assessment for
Middle and High School Classrooms
Deborah Blaz

Handbook on Differentiated Instruction
for Middle and High Schools
Sheryn Spencer Northey

Differentiating Assessment in Middle and High School
Mathematics and Science
Sheryn Spencer Waterman

Differentiating Assessment in Middle and High School
English and Social Studies
Sheryn Spencer Waterman

Formative Assessment for English Language Arts
A Guide for Middle and High School Teachers
Amy Benjamin

Supplemental Downloads

The implementation tools and discussion questions in this book are also available on Eye On Education's Web site as Adobe Acrobat files. Permission has been granted to purchasers of this book to download these resources and print them.

You can access these downloads by visiting Eye On Education's Web site: www.eyeoneducation.com. From the home page, click on FREE, then click on Supplemental Downloads. Alternatively, you can search or browse our Web site to find this book, then click on "Log in to Access Supplemental Downloads."

Your book-buyer access code is **AMH-7233-8.**

Index of Supplemental Downloads

Contents

Acknowledgements

Several of my colleagues provided critical support in editing: Ashley Taylor, Melissa Rudloff, Jennifer Gonzalez, Marge Maxwell, and Keri Mosier. Also, Janet Tassell and Martha Day have previously collaborated with me in presenting and publishing on this topic. Without a network of committed and supportive colleagues, this work would not have been possible. Additionally, several teacher candidates and current teachers—Josh Bush, Chloe Harper, Nicholas Neiman, Hannah Blakenship, Natalie Croney, Jill Spears, Nathan Maness, Chelsea Elliot, Elliot Bracksierk, Kyle Marshall, Kacey Page, and Megan Steen—worked in partnership with me to create the assessments in this text. Finally, I am thankful to my husband as well as my parents, who have always supported my aspirations.

Meet the Author

Rebecca Stobaugh received a PhD from the University of Louisville. As a middle-school and high-school teacher, she was named Social Studies Teacher of the Year by the Kentucky Council for Social Studies in 2004. In her position as a middle-school principal, she focused on aligning curriculum, increasing the level of critical thinking in assessments and instruction, and establishing a school-wide discipline plan. Currently, she serves as an assistant professor at Western Kentucky University, teaching assessment and unit-planning courses in the teacher education program. She supervises first-year teachers and consults with school districts on critical thinking, instructional strategies, assessment, technology integration, and other topics.

Introduction: Engaging in Critical Thinking

Whether it is a problem with your car, a neighbor, or your job, situations in life present complex challenges that demand critical thinking to carefully examine the situation and formulate a solution. Memorized terms do not prepare us for these problems. In order to be primed for adult life, students need experience engaging in higher-level thinking tasks and assessments.

Critical thinking skills should be infused into daily instruction to adequately prepare students for school assessments, rigorous college expectations, employers' demands, and complex life situations. Equipping students with critical thinking skills enables them to reason effectively, make rational judgments and decisions, and solve problems.

Since there are many misconceptions about levels of thinking, this book initially delves deeper into the revised Bloom's cognitive taxonomy to build greater understanding of each level and its cognitive processes. Next, it addresses prevailing misconceptions about critical thinking and problems associated with trying to design high-level thinking tasks and assessments. A solution will then be provided to increase the level of cognitive complexity in instructional tasks and assessments—using interpretive exercises. The next three chapters demonstrate how to incorporate interpretive exercises by using quotes, visuals, and scenarios. Finally, ideas will be shared on how to establish a culture of thinking in a classroom along with techniques to embed interpretive exercises into formative and summative assessments. At the end of each chapter are discussion questions, ways to make practical applications, and supplementary resources. Reading this text will equip middle and high school educators with knowledge and skills to develop high-level thinking tasks and assessments.

The first chapter defines critical thinking and establishes the importance of infusing critical thinking skills into instruction. Teaching critical thinking skills prepares students for P-12 assessments, rigorous college expectations, employers' demands, and complex life situations. Equipping students with critical thinking skills enables students to reason effectively, make rational judgments and decisions, and solve problems.

Since there are many misconceptions on levels of thinking, this book in the second chapter initially delves deeper into the revised Bloom's cognitive taxonomy (Anderson & Krathwohl, et al., 2001) to build greater understanding of each level and its' cognitive processes. Vignettes are provided at the beginning of each cognitive process to showcase real-life examples of the cognitive dimensions. In addition, numerous examples of instructional tasks and assessments at each level are identified.

The third chapter identifies prevailing misconceptions associated with the taxonomy and problems associated with trying to design high-level thinking tasks and assessments. Using interpretive exercises is presented as one solution to increase the level of cognitive complexity in instructional tasks and assessments.

Scenarios, real-world examples, and authentic tasks are described in the fourth chapter as a method to assess students in realistic contexts. Descriptions of scenarios, real-world examples, and authentic tasks are provided along with an explanation of how these can be used to boost higher-level thinking. This chapter also includes design tips and numerous examples from a variety of subject areas.

In Chapter 5, using visuals is identified as a method to increase the thinking levels in assessment. Visuals include illustrations, maps, diagrams, data tables, and charts that appeal to visual learners while also engaging them in higher-level thinking. This chapter describes each of these types of pictorial representations and how they can be integrated in instructional tasks and assessments. Design tips are included along with numerous examples from a variety of subject areas.

In Chapter 6, short quotes, passages, and media clips are presented as another approach to challenge students to understand, analyze, and evaluate information. The text describes ways to utilize quotes, passages, and media clips in instruction and assessment while addressing how they can enhance higher-level thinking. Design tips are included along with numerous examples from a variety of subject areas.

Chapter 7 showcases ways to build a thinking culture in a classroom along with ideas to embed interpretive exercises into formative and summative assessments. The final chapter summarizes the text and directs the reader to establish a plan with specific goals to implement the ideas presented in the text. By learning the knowledge and skills to develop high-level thinking tasks and assessments, middle and high school educators will be more prepared to lead classrooms where students engage in meaningful learning experiences.

This book provides middle and high school educators with the knowledge and skills they need to develop high-level thinking tasks and assessments. There is a companion volume available for elementary school educators, *Assessing Critical Thinking in Elementary Schools: Meeting the Common Core.*

Importance of Critical Thinking

To succeed in the 21st century, all students will need to perform to high standards and acquire mastery of rigorous core subject material. All students also will need to gain the cognitive and social skills that enable them to deal with the complex challenges of our age.
                    —The Partnership for 21st Century Skills

When I was a principal, one day the cafeteria manager reported that a student threw a strawberry during lunch. The student vehemently denied committing such an atrocious offense. Therefore, I conducted further interviews with students sitting at his table and near where the strawberry landed. All the stories pointed toward the accused student as the culprit. I asked the strawberry thrower to please clean up the table and floor where the strawberry was thrown. After several requests he adamantly refused to clean up the area, so I assigned him to the alternative learning area for the rest of the day. His guardian was informed of the incident. Several hours later I heard yelling in the front office, and the secretary informed me that the strawberry thrower's mother wanted to speak to me. I invited her back to my office to discuss the incident. I tried to explain how I had investigated the situation; however, she refused to sit down and proceeded to defend her child, insisting that he would never throw anything. My attempts to calm her down were futile. Holding her cell phone up in the air with fingers on the numbers, she finally shrieked, "I am going to call 911!" At that moment I just stood looking at her, not knowing how to proceed. Although I had enjoyed an excellent undergraduate and graduate education, I did not remember anything in my coursework suggesting how to handle an irate mom calling 911 over a strawberry tossed across the lunchroom. I suspect even Google couldn't have helped me here.

I felt sure that there was some piece of information that I was not connecting. I calmly asked her why this incident was making her so upset. After de-escalating this situation for a few minutes through rational conversation, I was able to piece together that she was angry that her son would be missing a field trip the next day due to being in the alternate learning classroom. As a compromise we agreed that instead of missing the field trip, the mother and son would clean the lunchroom together. This solution satisfied the mother because her son could go on the field trip, and I knew that cleaning the lunchroom would teach him the value of hard work and hopefully increase his respect for the school facilities. Interestingly, I never saw the offending student in the office again for misbehavior.

Life is complex. We all face similar situations where understanding complicated issues is critical to addressing the problem. The workplace and the world are rapidly evolving with abundant information and massive technological advances. How can we prepare our students to rapidly and successfully adapt to the changing world and complex circumstances they will encounter? We teach them to think! Thinking skills should be infused into daily instruction to adequately prepare students for college, careers, and life. Without these skills, students cannot effectively analyze multiple sources of information, draw logical conclusions, and create new innovations.

What Is Critical Thinking?

It is easy to define what critical thinking is not—a memorized answer or reactive thinking. Critical thinking is not a simplistic recalling of previous information or illogical and irrational thinking. Reactive thinking is instinctive.

People who disdain critical thinking often jump to conclusions, fail to recognize biases, and are unwilling to consider various perspectives. Weak critical thinkers address a problem or challenge by failing to understand and organize the important facts of the situation, being distracted by unimportant information, lacking perseverance to solve the problem, and designing a vague solution, not appropriate to the specific situation (Facione, 2011). Do you know people like this? All people have times in their lives when they might exhibit some characteristics of weak critical thinkers.

There are various definitions of critical thinking. According to Chaffee (1988), critical thinking is "our active, purposeful, and organized effort to make sense of our world by carefully examining our thinking, and the thinking of others, in order to clarify and improve our understanding" (p. 29). Critical thinking is analytical and deliberate and involves original thinking. Critical thinking is deeply processing knowledge to identify connections across disciplines and find potential creative solutions to problems. Critical thinkers use reflective decision-making and thoughtful problem-solving to analyze situations, evaluate arguments, and draw appropriate inferences. Critical thinkers have a passion to seek the truth even when the truth may contradict long-held beliefs.

Figure 1.1   **21st Century Critical Thinking Skills**

Reason Effectively
◆ Use various types of reasoning (inductive, deductive, etc.) as appropriate to the situation

Use Systems Thinking
◆ Analyze how parts of a whole interact with each other to produce overall outcomes in complex systems

Make Judgments and Decisions
◆ Effectively analyze and evaluate evidence, arguments, claims and beliefs ◆ Analyze and evaluate major alternative points of view ◆ Synthesize and make connections between information and arguments ◆ Interpret information and draw conclusions based on the best analysis ◆ Reflect critically on learning experiences and processes

Solve Problems
◆ Solve different kinds of non-familiar problems in both conventional and innovative ways ◆ Identify and ask significant questions that clarify various points of view and lead to better solutions

Source: From The Partnership for 21st Century Skills (2011). *21st century critical thinking skills.* Copyright 2013 Eye On Education, Inc. Reprinted with permission of The Partnership for 21st Century Skills.

The Partnership for 21st Century Skills (2011) has identified four areas of critical thinking skills: (1) reasoning effectively, (2) using systems thinking, (3) making judgments and decisions, and (4) solving problems. (See Figure 1.1.) These thought processes often require students to examine multiple information sources and identify the key information relevant to the task. Critical thinkers often possess a probing inquisitiveness, zealous dedication to understanding, eagerness to obtain reliable information or evidence, and purposeful, reflective judgment based on consideration of evidence. To make informed decisions and evaluate the impact of actions, critical thinkers use multiple thought processes at once. To teach students how to appropriately approach multifaceted problems, questions, and decisions, schools must design curriculum that replicates the complicated nature of the real world. With cognitively demanding instructional tasks, classrooms can promote an intellectually stimulating learning environment that prepares students for the 21st century.

Importance of Critical Thinking

Global changes are directly impacting education. With increasingly complex jobs, global interdependence, and technological advances, the expectations for workforce skills are evolving. Workforce demands are leaving low-skilled workers with few options for other careers. Life choices are complex due to the proliferation of a variety of information that can be inaccurate and biased.

Without refined critical thinking skills, erroneous information can negatively impact life decisions. In order to counteract these changes, students must be equipped with thinking skills to deliberately examine information and make logical decisions.

Several benefits arise from practicing and refining students' critical thinking skills. Embedding critical thinking skills in the curriculum helps sustain an educated citizenry; prepares students for college, future careers, and life situations; and primes students to meet mandates of state and national tests and standards.

Sustaining Democracy

Thinking skills are vital in sustaining a democratic government. When citizens utilize critical thinking, countries can make good judgments about the best course of action. With critical thinking skills, individual citizens can effectively examine various candidates for election, decide how to act if they disagree with government measures, and carefully review opposing evidence as a jury member and make a sound decision based on facts. Since education is the primary means for preparing students to be citizens, schools should focus on embedding these skills in instructional tasks and assessments. Schools have the job of inculcating these skills in all students in order to prevent democracies from being led by the elite. Maintaining a democracy requires that all citizens possess an ability to critically engage in democratic functions.

College, Career, and Life Success

The Partnership for 21st Century Skills (2011) advocates merging the 3Rs (core academic content mastery) and the 4Cs (critical thinking and problem-solving, collaboration, communication, and creativity and innovation). (See Figure 1.2.) Fusing these skills together can prepare students for success in college, career, and life. While students may forget the specific content of their classes, critical thinking is a skill that prepares them to adapt to changing circumstances in the 21st century.

College Success

High schools have been criticized for not adequately preparing students for the level of rigor they will encounter in college (Achieve, 2006). The ACT test, which is used as a measure of college and career readiness, defines if students will be able to be successful in first-year courses at a postsecondary institution without the assistance of remediation courses. ACT's College Readiness Benchmarks define minimum scores needed on the ACT subject area tests to predict a 50 percent chance of obtaining a B or higher or a 75 percent chance of obtaining a C or higher in a first-year college course. In 2011, 66 percent of high-school graduates taking the ACT met the English College

Figure 1.2 Partnership for 21st Century Skills: Framework for 21st Century Learning

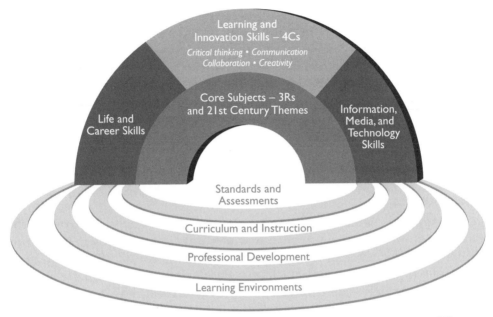

21st Century Student Outcomes and Support Systems

Source: From The Partnership for 21st Century Skills (2011). *Partnership for 21st century skills: Framework for 21st century learning.* Copyright 2013 Eye On Education, Inc. Reprinted with permission of The Partnership for 21st Century Skills.

Readiness Benchmark. Twenty-five percent successfully passed all four College Readiness Benchmarks. Twenty-eight percent of high-school students did not pass any of the College Readiness Benchmarks. ACT reports that these test scores remained essentially the same between 2007 and 2011 (ACT, 2011). ACT predictions have been confirmed: nearly one-third of students entering some type of postsecondary education take remedial courses in one or more subjects because they lack the skills to take standard credit-bearing courses (National Center for Education Statistics, 2011).

ACT research shows a positive benefit of a rigorous core preparatory curriculum for all students. A rigorous curriculum would include foundational skills that adequately prepare students for college-level work. The *Ready to Succeed* report states, "Students enrolled in such a curriculum earn higher scores on the ACT, are better prepared to enter the workplace and/or credit-bearing college courses, show increased persistence in postsecondary education, and have significantly greater chances of earning college degrees and succeeding in the workplace" (ACT, 2006, p. 2).

Increasing the level of critical-thinking skills in any program raises the level of rigor. Critical thinking has been cited as a key factor in student success in college. In a study of college seniors, students' level of critical thinking was predictive of their cumulative college grade point average (Torres, 1993). In a study to examine thinking skills, including problem-solving and creativity, Sternberg (2008) gave tests to college freshmen and high-school seniors. The findings showed that this test predicted students' grades as college freshmen twice as well as SAT scores and high-school grade point averages. Similarly, in a study of 1,100 college students, critical-thinking tests significantly correlated with college grade point averages (Facione, 1990a, 1990b). In 2011, a research study surveyed teachers, parents, students, and Fortune 100 executives to determine what were the key areas to prepare students for college and career readiness. Two areas emerged with 90 percent agreement among all groups: problem-solving skills and critical-thinking skills (MetLife, 2011). Therefore, embedding critical-thinking experiences into the school curriculum can have a positive impact on students' potential for college success.

Career Success

Critical-thinking skills are imperative in any job. Doctors are expected to listen carefully to a patient's account of medical ailments, review prior conditions, consider medical knowledge, and utilize prior experiences to treat the condition accurately and efficiently. Possessing critical-thinking skills is required for professional positions. Employers expect that their employees use reasoned judgment. One superintendent I know commented that the number-one quality that he desired in a principal is common sense when approaching complex problems.

The Conference Board (2006) conducted a survey of human resource professionals and found that 70 percent of employees with a high-school education were lacking in critical-thinking skills. This statistic is worrying considering that routine jobs are increasingly being replaced by computerized machines. Basic skills hence are insufficient for job survival. Businesses want workers who utilize critical-thinking skills for decision-making, independent thinking, and problem-solving (Silva, 2008). For example, hotel front-desk clerks used to provide check-in services; however, now some hotels provide online check-in. Front-desk clerks are evolving, as are employees in many other careers, into workers who use their critical-thinking abilities to solve customers' problems. Businesses expect that even workers who move from high school directly into the workforce need to possess critical-thinking skills to handle a myriad of challenges they will encounter.

With the global economy, low-skill jobs are moving to other countries with cheaper labor forces. In order for the United States to maintain the high-skill positions, it must have an educational system that will prepare students for the new economy where rapid change demands that workers think and innovate. Workers are increasingly expected to collect information from various sources and to critically interpret information. The National Center on Education and the Economy (2008) states, "creativity and innovation are the keys to the good life, in which high levels of education—a very different kind of education than most of us have had—are going to be the only security there is" (p. 24). Employees are more valuable if they can solve problems and reason thoughtfully. To prepare students to meet employers' expectations, schools have a responsibility to provide multiple opportunities for students to enhance their thinking skills, deal with abstractions, and innovate.

Life Success

Have you heard a teenager talking about purchasing a car based on only the model and color without considering other important details like the quality of the engine? I am sure we all can remember instances in our lives when we failed to use sound thinking. I am embarrassed to say that I too failed to employ critical-thinking skills appropriately when I selected a boyfriend in high school. My criteria were limited to one—essentially, did he have a car? Surely, you recall similar decisions that lacked good thinking.

Poor thinking can result in bad decisions affecting not just ourselves but people around us. Failing to utilize critical-thinking skills causes many negative consequences: job loss, academic failure, financial problems, and family violence. Failing to consider financial decisions thoughtfully can lead to frivolous purchases and bankruptcy. Students settle for low-skill jobs that allow them to begin earning money quickly because they fail to understand the potentially higher earnings they can get with a specialized degree.

How many of our students are not prepared to make good choices in life because they have not learned to examine the details of the situation, clarify the problem, eliminate extraneous information, generate a list of good solutions, and select the best option? If all our students were good at this, there would be fewer disciplinary referrals. Life is about complex choices: selecting a career, choosing among housing options, and sometimes selecting a mate. In essence, critical thinking is essential for survival and self-sufficiency. It moves students from intellectual dependence to independence.

National Standards

The importance of critical thinking is noted in the new national standards. The Common Core State Standards (CCSS) Initiative directly identifies higher-order thinking skills as critical to achieving career and college readiness for all students. To meet the demand for students to be college and career ready, the language arts standards identify the following behaviors of a 21st-century literate person:

> [Students] habitually perform the critical reading necessary to pick carefully through the staggering amount of information available today in print and digitally.... They reflexively demonstrate the cogent reasoning and use of evidence that is essential to both private deliberation and responsible citizenship in a democratic republic. (National Governors Association Center for Best Practices, 2010a, p. 3)

This vision for the Common Core State Standards clearly shows the emphasis on deep-thinking tasks. Similarly, the first three Common Core State Standards of mathematical practice are to "Make sense of problems and persevere in solving them," "Reason abstractly and quantitatively," and "Construct viable arguments and critique the reasoning of others" (National Governors Association Center for Best Practices, 2010b, p. 6). All these mathematical standards embody cognitively demanding tasks. As educators pursue CCSS alignment, then, it is crucial to design curricula and assessment systems that emphasize authentic real-world problems, engage students in inquiry and exploration, and provide opportunities for students to apply what they know in meaningful ways.

Preparation for State and National Tests

High-stakes testing has intensified the accountability of teachers and schools. More and more national assessments are embedding critical-thinking questions; for example, the SAT now includes an analytic essay. Punitive sanctions and negative reports to the public due to low student achievement have caused schools to examine curriculum and assessments carefully to ensure they are aligned to state and national standards both in the content and in the level of thinking required. Cognitively demanding tasks provide the means to equip students to learn well. Shepard (2001) advocates for standards-based reform with challenging curriculum for all students focused on higher-order thinking skills and deep conceptual understanding.

Critical thinking promotes academic growth. In fact, intentionally teaching thinking skills is associated with increased test scores (Wenglinsky, 2000, 2002, 2003). Learning targets, strategies, and assessments requiring higher levels of cognitive thinking have been found to positively impact student learning (Raths, 2002). Furthermore, research shows that SAT scores significantly correlate with scores on critical-thinking instruments in numerous studies (Facione, Facione, & Giancarlo,1992; Jacobs, 1995; Frisby, 1992), as do ACT scores (Mines, King, Hood, & Wood, 1990; King, Wood, & Mines, 1990). When critical thinking skills are integrated into instruction, students will possess a deeper-level understanding of concepts (Swartz & Parks, 1994). This deeper level of understanding helps students perform at a higher level on state and national tests. Though critical-thinking tasks may take longer for students to complete due to the time to process one's thinking, schools focusing on reasoning and thinking skills will reap the benefits with higher test scores.

Student Motivation

Recently, a high-school teacher that previously attended one of my trainings contacted me stating that her students were unmotivated. For several days in a row, her lessons included some fill-in-the-blank worksheets where students recorded definitions. She said that the assignments were easy, but several students were refusing to complete them. After listening to her account,

I suggested that perhaps students were not completing the assignments *because* they were simple. While some teachers make classroom activities easy in order to encourage students to complete the assignments, sometimes students see the assignment as not worth their time—mere busywork.

In *The Silent Epidemic* (Civic Enterprises, 2006), a report based upon responses from high-school dropouts, 66 percent of the dropouts said they would have given more effort to their work if their teachers had had higher expectations. According to Blackburn (2008), the idea that "students do not like hard work" is a misconception; "actually, students associate feelings of success and satisfaction with challenging work" (pp. 30, 31). Students notice busywork and respond in turn with low motivation, but when an authentic problem requires thinking skills, they are more motivated to complete the task. When teachers design cognitively complex assignments requiring students to analyze relationships and evaluate the best plans involving real-world topics, the students engage in the content in a meaningful and invigorating way. These instructional tasks actively engage students in complex problems while constructing meaning, a process that can transform students into attentive, eager, high-level thinkers.

Summary

People with refined critical-thinking skills are able to understand the world around them and make good decisions. These skills are absolutely critical for sustaining democratic governments, increasing levels of college preparedness, improving employability, making life decisions, performing on educational assessments, and increasing student motivation. Clearly, the benefits for integrating critical thinking into the curriculum are apparent. Our job as educators, then, is to create opportunities for students to develop and enhance these skills.

Understanding the importance of critical thinking is the first step. This text will examine various levels of thinking. Since there are many misconceptions about these levels, this book initially delves into the revised Bloom's cognitive taxonomy (Anderson &Krathwohl, 2001) to build understanding of each level and its cognitive processes. With a clear understanding of this framework, educators will be able to assess the level of thinking in their classrooms. The third chapter will identify prevailing misconceptions associated with the taxonomy and its implementation and provide a solution to increase the level of cognitive complexity in instructional tasks and assessments, using interpretive exercises. The successive three chapters demonstrate how to incorporate interpretive exercises using scenarios, visuals, and quotes. Finally, the seventh chapter shares ideas on how to establish a culture of thinking in a classroom along with techniques to embed interpretive exercises into formative and summative assessments. At the end of each chapter are discussion questions to spark thinking with colleagues in small groups, teams, or professional learning communities. Additionally, each chapter concludes with a *Take Action* section to assist teachers in making practical applications of the knowledge presented in each chapter. Resources, including rubrics, assessments, evaluation tools, and other materials, are included to support teachers in this work.

Discuss

♦ What do you think is the most compelling reason for students to be taught critical thinking?

♦ What is the most important reason to include critical-thinking skills in your curriculum?

♦ What are the consequences of *not* teaching critical thinking?

♦ Describe an example when a lack of critical thinking had a negative impact on your life.

Take Action

Using the assessment in Figure 1.3, Characteristics of Strong Critical Thinkers, rate your own and the average level of your students' critical thinking in your class.

1. How can you personally become a better critical thinker?

2. How can you raise the level of critical thinking in your classroom?

3. Which critical thinking attributes could you promote in your classroom instruction?

4. What activities would you use to integrate that attribute into your instruction?

Figure 1.3 **Characteristics of Strong Critical Thinkers**

Rate yourself and the general level of class critical thinking skills. Assign a value from 1 to 10 to each critical thinking attribute, with higher numbers used to show which attributes best describe you.

Self Assessment	Class Assessment	
		Inquisitiveness with regard to a wide range of issues
		Concern to become and remain well-informed
		Alertness to opportunities to use critical thinking
		Self-confidence in one's own abilities to reason
		Open-mindedness regarding divergent world views
		Flexibility in considering alternatives and opinions
		Understanding of the opinions of other people
		Fair-mindedness in appraising reasoning
		Honesty in facing one's own biases, prejudices, stereotypes, or egocentric tendencies
		Prudence in suspending, making, or altering judgments
		Willingness to reconsider and revise views where honest reflection suggests that change is warranted

Source: Adapted from Insight Assessment. (n.d.). *Characteristics of strong critical thinkers.* Copyright 2013 Eye On Education, Inc. Reprinted with permission of Insight Assessment.

Applying Bloom's Taxonomy in Your Classroom

Thinking leads man to knowledge. He may see and hear, and read and learn, as much as he pleases; he will never know any of it, except that which he has thought over, that which by thinking he has made the property of his mind. Is it then saying too much if I say, that man by thinking only becomes truly man? Take away thought from man's life, and what remains?
— Johann Heinrich Pestalozzi

Critical thinking as applied to K–12 schools was foundationally established in 1956 when Benjamin Bloom edited the text titled *Taxonomy of Educational Objectives* (Bloom, 1956). This handbook established a taxonomy or classification system for cognitive objectives. Bloom's work was recognized by teachers, administrators, and curriculum specialists as a way to examine the degree of thinking in classrooms. The taxonomy included six levels: Knowledge, Comprehension, Application, Analysis, Synthesis, and Evaluation.

With new understandings about education, in 2001 the framework was revised by a group who worked for five years to clarify the taxonomy (Anderson & Krathwohl, 2001). The dimensions on the taxonomy are similar, but the highest two levels on the framework have been interchanged. Evaluation is now the fifth level and Creation, previously termed Synthesis, is at the top level of the taxonomy. In the 2001 framework, the dimensions also shifted to verb form to indicate the cognitive skill expected at each level. The levels now are Remember, Understand, Apply, Analyze, Evaluate, and Create. The revised version identifies significantly more cognitive processes under each level to clarify the level of thinking in each category. The revised taxonomy includes nineteen cognitive processes classified in six categories. Previously it was considered that basic levels of understanding must be mastered before higher levels could be addressed. Now, on many occasions students may begin even at the highest level of Create and learn low-level knowledge while engaging in a high-level thinking assignment.

Figure 2.1 **Changes in Bloom's Taxonomy Cognitive Levels**

Retention versus Transfer

Educators have long discussed the importance of transferring new knowledge versus simply retaining information for the short term. Retention is the ability to recall information at a later time in a similar situation. Transfer is the ability to utilize previously learned information or skills in a new situation (Mayer & Wittrock, 1996). Retention involves recalling facts, like the definition of a tragedy. While facts can be memorized, recalling facts alone cannot solve unfamiliar or complex problems. Recalling facts is represented on the lowest levels of Bloom's taxonomy. Robert Reich (1989) characterized the education system as an assembly line, where students learn "long lists of facts that 'every adult should know' and standardized tests produce robots adept at Trivial Pursuit but unable to think for themselves or to innovate for the future" (p. 100).

Teaching to make sure students retain information is very different from teaching for transfer. Teaching students to make meaningful connections and transfer requires that students engage in cognitively demanding tasks at the higher levels of Bloom's taxonomy. The benefit of this level of learning is that it is preserved in the memory for longer periods of time; students can use information to determine answers to test questions, apply concepts to work situations, and even make good life decisions. If students evaluate how characters approach tragic life circumstances in literature, for example, it could help them guide a friend on how to handle difficult circumstances in real life. When students are able to transfer learning to new situations, meaningful learning occurs (Anderson & Krathwohl, 2001).

Revised Cognitive Levels for Bloom's Taxonomy

As explained above, the revised Bloom's cognitive taxonomy includes six levels: Remember, Understand, Apply, Analyze, Evaluate, and Create. Subordinate cognitive processes are identified within each of the six levels to further describe the level of cognitive complexity. Bloom's cognitive levels and processes are summarized below. To clarify each cognitive process, vignettes of real-world instances and assessment examples are provided.

Level 1: Remember

Remembering, the first level of the taxonomy, involves retrieving information from the memory. At the Remember level the expectation is that the information is presented in some form and the student will retain it and be able to produce it later in a similar way as it was presented. A metaphor of the Remember level is a copy machine. Whatever the operator commands it to do, it does. The copy machine will not change the image unless directed to do so by the operator. The image is replicated exactly unless the operator instructs the machine to configure it another way. Students answer questions exceptionally well on this level because little thinking is required, only remembering.

Possessing factual knowledge is critical for higher levels of thinking. While memorizing the basic components of a sentence, a noun and a verb, is a Remember-level activity, without this knowledge writing would be an arduous task. Thus, Remember-level knowledge is a necessary foundation for more complex thought processes. In essence, a strong knowledge base allows students to effectively solve critical-thinking problems (Sternberg, 2008). There are two cognitive processes in the Remember level: Recognizing and Recalling.

Remember-Level Cognitive Process: Recognizing

An American highschool student visits Japan as an exchange student and comes to love a certain dish, tempura. Years later she tells her husband that this was her favorite dish. While visiting a Japanese restaurant, his wife exclaims "Oh, they have my favorite dish." Her husband immediately points to tempura on the menu.

In this vignette, the husband sees tempura on the menu and recognizes it as his wife's favorite dish because of an earlier conversation. Students' ability to recognize information after it has been presented, as in this scenario, is a low-level task. In the Recognizing level, the learner searches for the memorized answer in the information provided. To assess students' ability to recognize, teachers can use forced-choice or selected-response assessments such as multiple-choice, true-false, matching, or fill-in-the-blank questions. Another example: in a typing class, the teacher shows the students how to hold their hands on the keyboard. On the assessment, the teacher provides three pictures and the students must identify which one shows their hands in the correct typing position.

Classroom Example
Remember Level: Recognizing

In-class instruction:

Students memorize the definition of an associative property.

Assessment:

When adding more than two numbers, the grouping of the addends does not change the sum. Which property is described in the previous statement?

a. **associative property**

b. distributive property

c. commutative property

Remember-Level Cognitive Process: Recalling

While Joyce is eating at a restaurant, a former student comes to the table. "Hi, how are you? Do you remember me? You were my teacher in eighth grade."

Joyce stares at her. Six years have passed since she had this student in class and the girl's face and hair have changed considerably. "Oh, you were in the group that did the Civil War play. Weren't you? Yes, your name is Hannah."

"I can't believe you remember my name," Hannah says.

Joyce thinks to herself, "Me too," because sometimes recalling former students' names is a difficult endeavor.

Closely related to Recognizing, Recalling requires learners to remember relevant information to complete the task in an open-ended question or fill-in-the-blank assessment format. In this vignette, Joyce has to summon Hannah's name from her memory. Many teachers use this cognitive process when questioning. For example, a teacher states the definition of the term "evaporation." To check students' understanding, the teacher then asks students to recite the definition of the term. In this case, students are retrieving information from their memory. The game show *Jeopardy* represents thinking at this level. Many of the *Jeopardy* questions are difficult because they are obscure, but they do not require high levels of thinking because contestants are recalling information from memory.

Level 2:
Understand

At the Remember level, information can quickly be recalled from the brain's short-term memory, but without deeper thinking, information can be discarded without moving to the long-term memory. Students often memorize information to pass a test and a day later cannot retrieve the information. Teaching at the Remember level is like a spray of a water hose on a hot day. While you might get wet for a moment, in a few minutes the water evaporates. Life is not a Trivial Pursuit game in which recalling isolated facts will lead to success. To move beyond memorization and acquiring knowledge, the Understand level involves logical thinking. Knowing is different from understanding.

The Understand level is the beginning of original thinking. Students are not retrieving information memorized; they are building new connections in their minds. Just as a light bulb connects to the power source and produces light, at the Understand level students develop new understandings. Paul and Elder (2005) state, "There is no way to impact, transfer, or inject the system in the mind of another person in pre-fabricated form. It cannot be put on a mental compact disk and downloaded into the mind without an intellectual struggle" (p. 13). At the Understand level, students receive information in oral, written, or graphic form and make meaning of the information. Cognitive development is an active process whereby students construct meaning in their minds. As Paul and Elder further comment, "To begin to take ownership one needs to give voice to those basic concepts;—e.g., to state what the concept means in one's own words; to elaborate what the concept means, again in one's own words; and then to give examples of the concept from real-life situations" (p. 10). These ideas are represented at the Understand level.

At the Understand level and the other four higher levels of the taxonomy, examples or tasks must be novel to provide a new challenge for students. If the teacher asks students to summarize a passage and the student is later asked to produce the same summary again, the second time it is presented it will be at the Remember level, recalling previously stored information. Instead, the teacher should select new examples or novel tasks in order to present different stimuli to challenge student thinking and reach the Understanding and higher levels of Bloom's taxonomy.

The Understand level of thinking has seven cognitive processes, far more than the other levels. A tremendous amount of teaching and learning in schools is on this level as students build conceptual knowledge. During oral questioning, teachers ask students to summarize what others have stated, relate topics to their previous knowledge, provide additional examples of a concept or idea, and make connections between various concepts. All these ideas are encapsulated at the Understand level. The Understand level cognitive processes are Interpreting, Exemplifying, Classifying, Summarizing, Inferring, Comparing, and Explaining.

Understand-Level Cognitive Process: Interpreting

David enjoys smartphone technology and uses it to take lots of pictures of his family. At a meeting, Stacy starts viewing David's pictures.

"So Jordan played softball this year."

In the pictures there was no text. So how did Stacy draw that conclusion? David's daughter, Jordan, was wearing black shorts, a pink T-shirt emblazoned with the word "Sparklers," and a cap. Posed with her hand on her hip, she was smiling while holding a baseball bat. Stacy interpreted the picture by converting the visual image into words.

Interpreting involves changing information from one form to another. Students can convert text into pictures, graphics, music, and paraphrases. After reading a passage or listening to a speaker, students can create pictures that summarize the text (text to pictures). Students could also create a diagram to show the sequence of events in the story (text to graphics). After viewing a picture or graphic, students could explain what it means (picture or graphic to text). After reading a passage, students could paraphrase what was said in their own words (words to paraphrasing). Students could also put their information in musical form by imaginatively changing the lyrics of a song to represent the summary of the plot in a story or the summary of a historic culture (words to music). Another creative way is to have students use their body position or hand motions to represent a concept. For instance, students could create hand motions that represent vocabulary words.

Classroom Example
Understand Level: Interpreting

In-class instruction:

Students read in their textbook about the concept of democracy and paraphrase what the authors say about the term.

Assessment:

Create a picture that represents your conceptual understanding of democracy.

Understand-Level Cognitive Process: Exemplifying

At a faculty meeting, Ty says to his teaching partner, Julie, "Michael is really demure."

"Oh, there you go using those big words again," Julie comments. "What does that mean?"

"Well, he acts like Chad around others," Ty responds.

"Oh, so you're saying he's modest and reserved. It's might be because he's a new teacher. When I was a new teacher, I was demure too."

Another cognitive process within the Understand level is Exemplifying. Students are often asked to provide another example of a concept; that is Exemplifying. In the vignette, the word "demure" is connected to another faculty member who acts in a similar fashion. By giving an example, Ty clarifies the meaning of the term. The following are some Exemplifying activities:

◆ Social studies: After discussing ancient Greek democracy, students provide a situation in their life where they see similar democratic principles at work.

◆ Language arts: While reading a book, students examine the concept of theme in the text. To assess their understanding of theme, students describe a fairy tale that has a similar theme or, in a multiple-choice format, select the title of another text they have already read that has a similar theme.

◆ Science: After studying examples of water conservation, students describe another way they can conserve water at home.

In their examples, students might be asked to provide another instance of the concept from within the discipline, another discipline, or their life. Challenging students to make connections across disciplines and to their life or prior knowledge builds greater meaning for students.

In-class instruction:

Students read about compounds and list H_2O as an example of a compound.

Assessment:

Which of the following is a compound?

    a. potassium (K)

    b. salt (NaCl)

    c. iron (Fe)

    d. copper (Cu)

In this case, none of the choices above were listed in the text or discussed prior to the assessment.

Understand-Level Cognitive Process: Classifying

You receive an email that appears to be from the district office. The email discusses the district email system and then states that your email account is over capacity and that, in order to continue to use the system, you will need to provide the sender with your last name and password. This last part seems suspicious so you forward the email to your administrator because it seems to be a scam.

Classifying involves categorizing information or items based on similar characteristics. In the vignette above, the teacher recognizes attributes of a scam email message, particularly the request for the teacher's password, and thus classifies the message as a scam. Instead of taking a general concept and thinking of an example, as in Exemplifying, Classifying requires students to identify the key traits first and then determine the concept. Students engage in active cognitive processing by attending to stimuli and organizing information into meaningful chunks (Mayer, 1999). Chunking or grouping helps learners understand how items are alike and different.

The teacher can establish the categories and have students group information into those identified headings. For example, after listening to various musical pieces, students group the pieces by style. Additionally, a teacher might show a new instrument from another country and have students explain which musical family this instrument would fit into. In social studies, the students could read primary sources about early colonists and their environment and determine which region they lived in based on clues from the texts.

Classroom Example
Understand Level: Classifying

In-class instruction:

Students read about the differences between chemical and physical changes. Two examples of chemical and physical changes are provided in the text.

Assessment:

Students group examples in categories based on whether they involve chemical or physical changes.

Understand-Level Cognitive Process: Summarizing

Ms. Kim says to the class, "For tonight's homework, please read the chapter, noting the key vocabulary, and complete the assigned questions."

Juan, who was texting under his desk and didn't hear the instructions, taps Tarin sitting in front of him and asks, "What's the homework?"

Annoyed that she is repeating the directions, Tarin quickly says, "Read the chapter and do the questions."

Summarizing requires students to create a statement to represent a body of information. When we are asked to repeat information, we often simplify the message and summarize for the purpose of efficiency, as shown in the vignette. Teachers often use this strategy to assess students' understanding of the key points in the lesson. Teachers ask students to summarize by writing a three-word summary, compose a text message of less than thirty characters, develop a headline for a news article about the lesson, or read a journal article and write a title for it. Students could read, watch a video clip, or observe a natural event and summarize what happened. Students could also select, in a multiple-choice format, which statement best summarizes an information source. Students can use web technologies including Animoto, Glogster EDU, or Photo Peach to create short presentations integrating pictures and text to summarize information. To encourage artistic abilities, teachers can ask students to draw or paint a picture to summarize text.

Classroom Example
Understand Level: Summarizing

In-class instruction:

Students read about the impressionist art movement.

Assessment:

Which statement summarizes the ideas presented in the text on impressionist art?

    a. The impressionist art movement started in France as a reaction against traditional art and its strict rules.

    b. Impressionism covers a period from the late 1860s through the 1880s.

    c. A group of painters gained independence from the standards prescribed by the French Academy of Fine Arts.

    d. A French art critic, Louis Leroy, first used the term "impressionist."

Understand-Level Cognitive Process: Inferring

José never seems to complete homework. Mr. Frank wonders what could be the cause of this behavior: family challenges, lack of interesting assignments, or maybe assignments that are too easy or too hard. When the math class begins studying ellipses and parabolas, Mr. Frank assigns a real-life math problem to find the trajectory of a space launch based on the given information. Unexpectedly, José completes his homework and wants to discuss the assignment. To reinforce the learning, Mr. Frank provides another assignment requiring students to find the trajectory of a meteorite that could potentially crash to Earth. The next day in class, José again has his assignment completed and poses questions about other connections to space topics. Though Mr. Frank knows there are obviously many reasons for José's behavior, he concludes there seems to be a connection between his motivation to complete homework assignments and space topics.

Inferring is looking for a pattern or relationship between examples. Inferences can involve the use of inductive and deductive reasoning. Inductive reasoning establishes a sensible generalization from information supplied or reasons from the specific to a broader lens. For example, after a first day in your class, a student might conclude you are a dynamite teacher based on the introductory activity, your inviting classroom, and comments from previous students about your class. This use of inductive reasoning moves from general reasoning to the specific, as shown in the vignette. Mr. Frank starts with several potential reasons for the student's low motivation and eventually rules out several ideas after observing José's behavior.

People make inferences all the time. The process is so automatic that most of the time the brain immediately takes observations and begins putting the pieces together to draw conclusions. When inferences are based on limited proof, inaccurate conclusions can be drawn—for example, first impressions of people, based on their style of dress, body language, and speech, which due to inadequate evidence may or may not be accurate.

In a classroom, students could examine the motives for a person's actions. Students would list possible causes and then select the best reasons for the person's action. It is important that inferences be clear, logical, justifiable, and reasonable. Factual information is used to form a reasonable conclusion, but inferring means going beyond this information to understand knowledge in another area. Students utilize information from data, statements, evidence, situations, hypotheses, judgments, and other sources to draw reasonable inferences and conclusions.

Before learning about the proper usage of quotation marks, students could be given several sentences with quotation marks used in various ways. Students would then record the rules they infer for how to use quotation marks appropriately. Another way to provide opportunities for students to practice inferring is through analogy tasks. Analogy tasks require students to infer the relationship between objects, terms, or ideas. Students can examine the significant ways they are similar and make a conclusion about their connection.

Classroom Example
Understand Level: Inferring

In-class instruction:

Students examine input and output charts, identifying the rule.

Assessment:

Examine the input and output chart. Identify the rule.

Input	Output
2	12
8	48
11	66
Rule:	

    a. **multiply by 6**

    b. add by 10

    c. subtract by 10

    d. divide by 6

Understand-Level Cognitive Process: Comparing

It is time to renew your contract and select a new cell phone. To make a good decision, you search online to examine the features, prices, and available data plans of your two favorite phones.

Comparing involves examining two different items, situations, or ideas in order to identify the similarities or differences. Students might compare a literary figure to a present-day character in a film based on certain identified characteristics. Anderson and Krathwohl (2001) state, "Comparing includes finding one-to-one correspondences between elements and patterns in one object, event, or idea and those in another object, event, or idea" (p. 75). This strategy has been shown to have a powerful effect on learning (Marzano, Pickering, & Pollock, 2001).

Graphic organizers help students develop their comparisons by creating a chart with each comparison item as a column heading and the various categories for comparison as rows along the side of the chart. For example, students could compare soccer and basketball based on the rules, plays, penalties, and other areas. Or, students could create connection journals where they compare events in history to their lives, the world, or other texts. When students make connections to their lives, their level of interest in the task increases (Vosniadou, 2001).

Metaphors and analogies can be a way to show comparisons. Metaphors can show connections between two items that are typically not related. Using a topic studied, the teacher can give students the metaphor or students can write their own metaphor making connections between objects, persons, events, or ideas. Students can explain the key characteristics that make the one-to-one connections between the two items. Student comparisons might include a personal connection. For example, students could explain how photosynthesis is like cars using gasoline. Creating metaphors or analogies encourages imaginative thinking.

Classroom Example
Understand Level: Comparing

In-class instruction:

Students read about the current political parties.

Assessment:

Students should choose one current political party, select another political party not discussed in class, and then determine the similarities and differences between their platforms.

Understand-Level Cognitive Process: Explaining

"John, why did you knock her books out of her hand?" the principal asks. There is a long silence.

With head bowed, John says, "Because I like her."

"I see, but, John, didn't you notice when you do that she gets really angry with you?" the principal comments. "I think there might be other ways to get her attention that would help her like you more. Would you like to discuss some alternative options?"

Understanding means comprehending the basic cause-and-effect relationships. In this vignette, which occurs in middle schools many times, students attempt to flirt with other students and do not realize their attempts actually cause an opposite reaction from what they hoped. Explaining occurs when students make cause-and-effect connections between various ideas and concepts. It involves "constructing a cause-and-effect model, including each major part in a system or each major event in the chain, and using the model to determine how a change in one part of the system or one 'link' in the chain affects a change in another part" (Anderson & Krathwohl, 2001, p. 76). Sequencing or causal chains are taught with many concepts, such as the water cycle. Understanding the cyclical nature of certain systems helps to predict a reaction if one part of the cycle is interrupted. In English, characters in books display negative patterns of action that help readers predict the character's next action. By understanding the causal chain of events, students are able to comprehend the reason something happened and predict what might happen if similar instances occur. When working with cause-and-effect relationships, it is important to identify all contributory causes since in some instances there is more than one cause or multiple effects. If only one cause is considered, then the predicted effect might not be accurate.

Anderson and Krathwohl (2001) identify three areas for Explaining: troubleshooting, redesigning, and predicting. When troubleshooting, students encounter a problem and detect the cause of the problem. When redesigning, students examine the system and make changes to an identified purpose. When predicting, students think about how a change might impact other variables. Here are some examples of instructional tasks or assessment for troubleshooting, redesigning, and predicting:

- ◆ Troubleshooting: A new invasive plant, kudzu, has been found in our community growing along the sides of several roads. Describe what possible ways this plant may have arrived in our community.

- ◆ Redesigning: Fewer students are eating healthy snacks at school. How can the school encourage healthy snacks?

- ◆ Predicting: Describe the effects if the South had won the Civil War or if voter turnout at the polls continues to decline.

Classroom Example
Understand Level: Explaining

In-class instruction:
Students identify the key characteristics needed for an organism to survive in a particular ecosystem.

Assessment:
When given the description of a fictitious animal, students explain whether the animal will survive in a given ecosystem.

Level 3:
Apply

The third level of the revised cognitive taxonomy is Apply. In this level, there are certain procedures or steps that are expected to be followed to answer new problems. Thus, the teacher would model the appropriate steps to follow on an example and then students would follow a similar procedure to answer a different problem. There are two cognitive processes in the Apply level: Executing and Implementing. The Apply level is primarily connected to procedural knowledge because of the expected order or procedure to be followed, particularly in the Executing cognitive process; however, conceptual knowledge can be involved in the Implementing cognitive process.

Apply-Level Cognitive Process: Executing

Shopping—people either seem to like it or hate it. Jan loves to get a good deal and most of the time only browses the items on the discounted racks. She finds an item she would like to buy on a rack under a sign that states everything is 50 percent off. The item costs $20, so she computes half of its price would be $10.

In Executing, the student encounters a new example, but fairly quickly is able to see what procedure is needed. As in the scenario above, many people quickly calculate cost based on the percentage off. Computing this calculation is a routine skill using procedural knowledge taught in math classes. This cognitive process is well addressed in traditional math classes. The teacher models the procedure and then students complete additional problems repeating this method. For example, the teacher models how to solve problems using the quadratic formula. Students then apply the formula to different numbers and solve the equation. In science, the teacher models how to balance equations. Then students are asked to balance a new equation using the sequence the teacher just modeled. In an English class, students are taught how to appropriately use question marks. Students then receive a set of sentences and must correctly place the question mark at the end of each sentence. In social studies, students are taught how to find a specific location using longitude and latitude. Students then are given new points on a map and are expected to record the degrees of longitude and latitude for each location.

Classroom Example
Apply Level: Executing

In-class instruction:

Students are taught about commas and semicolons and how to use them appropriately in sentences.

Assessment:

Correct the sentence below with the correct punctuation.

1. I want to go with you mom said I could.

Apply-Level Cognitive Process: Implementing

At Moss Middle School, there is an exciting new teaching position posted you are interested in pursuing. The principal is a casual acquaintance. To pursue the position, it is recommended that you contact the principal. In high school, business letters and cover letters for resumes were clearly discussed. You write a letter, taking care to use a professional tone and format yet avoid being too formal and off-putting.

The Implementing cognitive process involves a murkier task than the Executing level. As in the example above, the casual acquaintance makes the task more challenging. Language that might be recommended in other business letters would not be appropriate for this situation due to the personal connection. At the Executing level, the procedure that should be applied is not readily apparent and the student must think through which procedure to select. The problem could be complex, with several possible answers. Often procedural and conceptual knowledge is required to complete the task. At the highest level of Implementing, the learner could use conceptual knowledge to establish a procedure for a task (Anderson and Krathwohl, 2001).

Here are some examples of Implementing tasks:

◆ Math: Students are presented with three options for a hypothetical summer vacation. Each option has discounts with special promotions. Students are to determine which trip is the best deal.

◆ Family and Consumer Science: After learning about several parental styles and the positives and negatives of each style, students watch a video segment showing a dysfunctional family. The students take the role of a therapist and identify what specific changes they would recommend to the family based on their previous knowledge of the various parental styles.

Classroom Example
Apply Level: Implementing Example

In-class instruction:

Students learn about Newton's three laws.

Assessment:

Students are asked to examine the information about a car crash and determine which if any of Newton's laws apply to the situation.

 Level 4:
Analyze

Analyze is the fourth level of the taxonomy. Just as a microscope takes a close view of each of the individual parts, the Analyze level involves breaking apart information to examine each section. The Analyze level requires students to utilize lower-level thinking skills, including the understandings, to identify the key elements first and then examine each part. Paul and Elder (2005) comments that high-performing students have the ability to accurately analyze problems and questions, as follows:

> [Students] gather information (distinguishing the relevant from the irrelevant), recognize key assumptions, clarify key concepts, use language accurately, identify (when appropriate) relevant competing points of view, notice important implications and consequences, and reason carefully from clearly stated premises to logical conclusions. (p. 15)

This describes many of the attributes of the Analyze level. The Analyze level is the foundation of higher-level skills on the Evaluate and Create levels (Anderson and Krathwohl, 2001). Often when the phrase "critical thinking" is used, it refers to the top three levels of Bloom's taxonomy: Analyze, Evaluate, and Create. A key component of critical thinking is the process of analyzing and assessing thinking with a view to improving it. Hence, many consider the Analyze level as the beginning of deep thinking processes. There are three cognitive processes in Analyze: Differentiating, Organizing, and Attributing. These three cognitive processes help students overcome some of the noted difficulties of thinking, including (a) impulsive conclusions, (b) failure to examine other points of view or identify assumptions, (c) unfocused or inexact thought processes, and (d) disorganized thinking (Perkins, 1995).

Analyze-Level Cognitive Process: Differentiating

"Mr. Harold, Mr. Harold!" said Summer. "I don't have my homework done today. Last night I had a softball game. We played Hopkinsville High School. It was a long trip. Did you hear about my hit? Oh, and our trip home was really long. Our bus driver did not know the roads very well. I worked on my homework on the way home, but Keri kept yelling and the road was bumpy. Have you ever been on that road to the school? It has some really bad twists and turns and major potholes ..."

Have you ever had a student approach you with a story like this? As teachers we are constantly engaging in the cognitive process of Differentiating, judiciously examining content for relevant and irrelevant characteristics. In the above example, many of the pieces of information mentioned by the student are not important to address the problem of the student not having her homework.

Do students know how to identify which information is important and relevant to a situation? A teacher told me she wanted to test her students' ability to discern which numbers in a math problem were relevant to create an equation. In her real-world math problem she included some irrelevant numbers. For example, "I'm going to put a fence around my square yard. I measured one side and it is 150 yards. I left my phone number (745-4438) with the fencing specialist. He called me back 30 minutes later and asked me about the type of fencing I would like. Based on the information provided, how much fencing do I need?" Would you be surprised to find out many students tried to use both the 30 (minutes) and the phone number in their calculations? Clearly, they were not able to identify relevant information. But when making real-world decisions, isn't relevant and irrelevant information often considered? Often students jump to conclusions without really examining pertinent evidence, as in the fencing problem. Paul and Elder (2005) state, "Thinking can only be as sound as the information upon which it is based" (p. 23). Therefore, students need to know which information is important for a given situation.

Discriminating information is critical to survival in the real world. Salespersons try to convince consumers to purchase items by including in their sales pitch irrelevant details that can distract consumers. To be informationally literate, students must possess this skill to know which information to consider and reject.

To practice discriminating between relevant and irrelevant information, students can read texts or listen to information sources that present irrelevant details. When students find extraneous information, they can mark it out or highlight key sections.

- ◆ Social studies: Students can listen to political speeches and identify the point of the speech and the related and unconnected details or examples that are used to support the main ideas.

- ◆ Language arts: When writing a research paper, students could create a list of sources that provide support for their thesis. In order to complete this task, students must be able to read each source and identify if it provides relevant information to support the thesis. Many sources may be discarded before the final list of sources is determined.

| **Classroom Example** |
| **Analyze Level: Differentiating Example** |
| In-class instruction:
Students read a student lab report and identify the evidence to support the finding. |
| Assessment:
Read the results of the scientific study and find supporting statements for each conclusion or finding. |

Analyze-Level Cognitive Process: Organizing

"Stop it," says nine-year-old Parker. "Ainsley's coming in my room and won't go away," he yells.

Hearing the commotion, the children's mother enters the room and asks what has happened. After hearing both sides explain what happened between Parker and his younger sister Ainsley, the mother is able to analyze the sequence of events to determine what really happened. She determines that Parker and Ainsley were kicking a ball. The ball hit Ainsley in the face, which caused her to get upset. To try to prevent her from getting more angry and telling on him, Parker started acting silly and tickling her. After she was in a better mood, Parker walked away to his room to play by himself. Ainsley, wanting to continue playing, repeatedly ran into Parker's room yelling childish phrases and quickly exiting, which annoyed him.

In the scenario above, the mother, through hearing both descriptions of the event, is able to sequence the events in order to examine the situation. With Organizing, students can create charts, diagram, flowcharts, other graphic organizers, or outlines to show connections among various pieces of information. With this cognitive process, students could construct charts to organize the key pieces of information, with varying designs from each student. Students could design organizers to show the multiple interactions occurring in a historical event, scientific results, and events in a reading. In a multiple-choice format, students could identify which organizer corresponds with the information source. An instructional strategy to practice this cognitive process is an inductive learning strategy: given a list of concepts, students group like concepts together by categorizing them and labeling what the concepts in the group have in common. With Organizing, students are grouping information together in a sensible way.

◆ Math: Students review math problems worked incorrectly and create a diagram to depict how the student who did the math is off track.

◆ Social studies: Students create an outline to depict the ideas present in the historical reading.

Classroom Example
Analyze Level: Organizing

In-class instruction:
Students scrutinize the plot structure of various novels.

Assessment:
After reading a new novel, students create a diagram to depict the key conflicts and their impact on plot development.

Analyze-Level Cognitive Process: Attributing

"Welcome to Fisher's! We have lots of cars to choose from here. What type of car would you like? Let me tell you about this car. It is very popular and affordable. We have payment plans .... Let's talk about your trade-in car. You'd be lucky to get a dollar for your car right now. But we'll give you $1,000. That's the book value. You can't believe the book values you see on Internet sites. Now let me tell you—this is a good deal. We're losing money on this deal!"

The world is filled with people trying to convince us to do or believe something. In our world, recognizing biases, assumptions, intentions, or points of view helps us critically examine information. It requires students to read between the lines—a step up from Inferring, an Understanding-level cognitive process. Often students examine information on the Internet without realizing that information posted online is not all credible. Many jobs require employees to examine information from various sources and identify the various biases and intentions.

With this cognitive process, students read or observe something and examine it to see if the information source has an underlying motive or bias. Many interest groups use persuasive messages to call for action. Students must be able to analyze various arguments and opinions presented while recognizing the perspectives presented. Students can discuss how various points of view can develop due to age, culture, social roles, employment, peer groups, religions, and gender.

Being open-minded to other viewpoints is often considered a trait of critical thinkers. Being open-minded means people are willing to consider divergent views and are aware of their own biases. An open-minded person respects the diverse opinions of others (Facione, 2011). Seeking information from divergent points of view and equally considering all viewpoints can help students with instructional tasks as well as conflict resolution, as parties are able to view information from various perspectives (Swartz & Parks, 1994). People have a natural tendency to favor their own position and interests while ignoring opposing arguments. With Attributing instructional tasks, students should be challenged to acknowledge their own assumptions and viewpoints that might involve prejudice, stereotypes, biases, and distortions. Assumptions are often (a) hidden or understated, (b) taken for granted, (c) influential in determining the conclusion, and (d) potentially deceptive (Browne & Keeley, 2004). By considering the assumptions of a writer or personal assumptions, students are able to analyze their own and others' thinking. Ultimately, the hope is to be able to judge objectively even if the conclusion is against their own self-interest.

For in-class experiences, students might analyze the various perspectives about a topic, considering opposing arguments and the reasons supporting each position. Any time various point of views are considered, classes can engage in healthy debate.

- ◆ Social studies: Students can examine historical writings to detect biases and points of view.

- ◆ Language arts: In *Charlotte's Web*, there are two clearly different points of view—the farmer's and the pig's. Students can pinpoint the perspectives and biases in the text.

- ◆ Math and science: Students can examine reports to determine the purpose for the data collection.

Classroom Example Analyze Level: Attributing
In-class instruction: Students investigate various forms of alternative energy sources.
Assessment: Upon reading articles from a variety of authors on solar energy, describe the differing viewpoints.

Level 5:
Evaluate

Evaluate is the fifth level of the taxonomy; typically the Analyze level and other lower cognitive processes are employed to engage in the Evaluate cognitive processes. In a courtroom, the judge makes a decision by weighing the evidence and deciding the best outcome or resources. At the Evaluate level, informational sources are examined to assess their quality and decisions are made based on the identified criteria. There are two cognitive processes in the Evaluate level: Checking and Critiquing.

Evaluate-Level Cognitive Process: Checking

The evidence is presented on both sides. One witness testifies for her mother and persuasively argues that her ex-husband hit her mother, causing major health problems. Health experts explain that the medical condition is due to blunt force trauma. The ex-husband clarifies that the mother refused to leave his house and, after an argument, he hit the mother. Now, it is the jury's responsibility to examine the facts.

Juries are expected to scrutinize information in order to determine if the witnesses are credible and if the testimony is accurate. Anderson and Krathwohl (2001) state, "Checking involves testing for internal inconsistencies or fallacies in an operation or product" (p. 83). A fallacy or internal inconsistency is an error in reasoning where the ideas in an argument do not adequately support the conclusion. Open-mindedness and considering alternative systems of thought are important, but students also need a critical eye when considering alternative views. Students possessing this cognitive ability pursue unsubstantiated claims, question ideas, and demand validation for arguments, interpretations, assumptions, beliefs, or theories.

When evaluating an argument, first the reader should determine the issue and/or conclusion. The conclusions and the reasons should support the argument. Evidence provides the proof, and the reasons explain why (Browne & Keeley, 2004). One way to help students to evaluate is to teach them to make sure viewpoints are supported with appropriate reasons and evidence. To introduce this skill, students can examine the arguments in a commercial, identifying the claim and deciding whether each claim is supported by reasons and evidence. Shel Silverstein's poem titled "Smart" is a good way to introduce incorrect assumptions. The boy in the poem trades his one dollar and collects more coins with each trade, but actually ends up with less money, five pennies. However, the child feels he has more now because he has more coins, even though the value of the coins is clearly less than the original amount.

Many students jump to conclusions or accept information without questioning the quality of the information. Students should practice evaluating information and sources. There are spoof websites that look deceptively real but have false information (Bradley, 2001). Using these sites in classroom instruction can teach students to carefully evaluate websites before using their information.

Many times on the news there are reports of new data. Are appropriate conclusions derived from the data? The common claim by students, "The teacher just doesn't like me" or by teachers, "Students just don't want to learn," can be a topic of conversation to engage students in this cognitive process. Students can examine the sources for credibility by assessing the reasonableness of ideas. Paul and Elder (2005) state that information should be examined based on its "clarity, accuracy, precision, relevance, depth, breadth, logic, and significance" (p. 12). There are many considerations when examining sources, including the following:

◆ **Author qualifications:** A work by an author should be considered a credible source if that author has a level of expertise in the area. However, even with that expertise, the source may have biases or special interests that distort the message. Additionally, evaluators should determine if the source is a primary or secondary account to assess the level of confidence that should be placed in the source.

◆ **Evidence:** A source should be supported by evidence. The reader should consider whether the evidence can be interpreted differently. The evidence should be accurate so as not to distort facts. Sometimes data are used inaccurately; thus the conclusions are inaccurate. When a conclusion or argument is posed, students should examine if the reasons provided support the idea. For example, in the magazine *Consumer Reports*, data are shown to support the recommendations.

◆ **Reliability of sources:** Evaluating the reliability of sources means considering whether other authorities agree. Even with a qualified author, more than one expert opinion can validate and corroborate information. Evaluators should determine if the source leaves out key information. The author may purposely include certain sources to support the message. For example, mass media and economic interests can spin messages to address their specific perspective. Also, with the rapidly changing information available, the date of publication can impact the reliability of the source (Chaffee, 2006).

To assess this cognitive process, students could conduct research on any topic and examine the print and media sources to evaluate whether the sources are credible and whether the conclusions are appropriately drawn from the informational source. Students might be able to draw other conclusions beyond what is mentioned. Most of these types of activities lead to essay or short-answer assessments.

◆ **English and social studies:** Students identify which source is the most reliable for a paper on election fraud.

◆ **Science:** Students examine if the sources used in a research report are appropriate and reliable.

Classroom Example
Evaluate Level: Checking

In-class instruction:
Students read about the physical effects of exercise on humans.

Assessment:
Read the article about a famous athlete. Identify one piece of information in the article that fails to support the author's case that hard work was the main reason for the athlete's exceptional athletic skills.

Evaluate-Level Cognitive Process: Critiquing

It's teacher evaluation time! You know the process. You will carefully prepare your lesson knowing an administrator will be evaluating you based on the state teacher standards. At the conclusion of the evaluation form, your strengths and areas for improvement are summarized.

Oh, a stressful time for teachers! Teacher evaluations are a good example of the Critiquing cognitive process. Critiquing involves assessing the value of an idea or product based on a set of criteria. The skill of decision-making is used in schools and in daily life to examine and then select from various choices (Sternberg, 2008). In schools, students seem to critique superficially almost every day as they state who is the best teacher (e.g., one that assigns no homework) or what car is the best to buy (e.g., of course, the one that is bright red). Without practice, students often rank choices based completely on personal preferences instead of developing logical criteria, thus making poor conclusions and decisions. Failing to build Critiquing skills leaves students unable to grapple with the complexities of life or to reasonably select the best option.

It seems the key decisions in life involve Critiquing, whether it is whom to marry, which house to purchase, or which career path to follow. Teaching students how to thoughtfully make reasoned decisions based on weighing the evidence prepares them for real-life situations they encounter. By learning how to evaluate, students can engage in healthy debates arguing a position, which many students enjoy doing. Students must examine the benefits, disadvantages, and potential consequences of each choice.

To reach this level, first the decision or problem must be defined along with the explicit criteria to evaluate the options. The decision could relate to a professional, personal, or civic problem. It could ask the students the "best" way to do something. What is the best way to solve a multistep real-world problem? Which is the best candidate for the position? The criteria might need to be researched to ensure proper considerations of key areas. Criteria can be based on the effectiveness of the solution, safety, cost-effectiveness, and other factors. Next, options or choices that align to the decisions should be identified. Students must be open-minded and willing to consider other ideas, options, and information in order to develop alternatives (Klaczynski, 2001). It is important to have a classroom climate that is supportive of divergent opinions and solutions so all options are considered. If the options are novel ideas, students could be working at the Create level using the Generating cognitive process, which will be introduced in the next section below. Next, students would explain with reasons how each option meets the criteria. Students might also rank the options or put the ideas on a continuum based on each idea meeting the criteria. Some criteria may be more important than others and thus be given more significant contemplation in ranking the alternatives. Some options might have important long- and short-term consequences to consider. If the options are not evaluated carefully with all pertinent information considered, decisions can be haphazard (Swartz & Parks, 1994). Finally, using convergent thinking, the best solution, idea, or product for a situation is selected.

Decision-Making Steps
1. Identify the problem or situation.
2. Secure relevant information.
3. Define criteria for evaluation.
4. Explore options.
5. Prioritize alternatives.

In schools, Critiquing exercises can be embedded in many areas. To prevent disciplinary infractions, school administrators often implore students to utilize this cognitive process to examine a course of action and whether it is effective. If Jack hits Mark, what are now the long-term consequences? What other options does a student have to deal with the conflict besides violence? Here are some other examples:

◆ **Math:** Students select which senior trip would be the best for students in their school based on established criteria and then develop a budget.

◆ **Language arts and social studies:** When studying historical figures or characters in a novel, students could identify who would be their friend based on criteria.

Another Critiquing instructional task is having students self-assess or peer-assess assignments according to the assignment rubric. This feedback can give students time to revise their assignment before turning it in for a grade while also compelling students to carefully read rubric expectations and utilize their higher-level thinking skills.

In-class instruction:

Students study the conflicts during the American Revolution.

Assessment:

Using primary sources, critique several American colonial actions that challenged the British government.

1. Develop criteria for evaluating the effectiveness of colonial actions in achieving colonial independence.

2. Select four colonial actions that showed the colonists' discontent with British government.

3. Using primary sources, explain how each action addressed each criterion for helping the colonists achieve independence.

Level 6:
Create

The final level of Bloom's taxonomy is the Create level. At this level learners are organizing information in a new or different way. This stage requires creative thinking. Silva (2008) states that "college students, workers, and citizens must be able to solve multifaceted problems by thinking creatively and generating original ideas from multiple sources of information" (p. 1). The need for creative thinking is also echoed by the Partnership for 21st Century Skills (2011), which considers creativity and innovation to be "some of the most important areas on which to focus CCSS (Common Core State Standards) work. In the 21st century, creativity and innovation skills are central components of college and career readiness" (p. 12).

The Create level has often been misunderstood. Creativity might involve designing a unique product, but it also includes combining various sources of information into a new product (Anderson and Krathwohl, 2001). Through the Create process, students will design a new product *different from the original materials*. According to Facione (2011), "*Creative* or *innovative thinking* [emphasis added] is the kind of thinking that leads to new insights, novel approaches, fresh perspectives, whole new ways of understanding and conceiving of things" (p. 14). This level could include solving a complex real-world problem or testing hypotheses through experimental inquiry. The product could be in the form of a presentation, paper, sculpture, or many other formats. However, "creating" a poster or website does not necessarily mean the task is at the Create level. As with all the Bloom's levels, teachers need to focus on how students are using the content in the class at a particular cognitive level (Maxwell, Stobaugh, & Tassell, 2012). For example, if students "created" a poster or website summarizing one of Shakespeare's plays, the task would be on the Understand level (Summarizing cognitive process). However, if students had to select a text that was at least 100 years old and market it to teens, this task would require creativity to think about the themes in the text and how they could appeal to students today. At the Create level, students must utilize the skills from lower levels of thinking, particularly Understand, Analyze, and Evaluate levels, as they seek to examine information and products already produced in order to determine the best way to design their product. At the Create level there are three cognitive processes: Generating, Planning, and Producing.

Create-Level Cognitive Process: Generating

> *A local community wants to honor the soldiers who have served in the military and positively impacted the community for many years. Community members brainstorm a list of possible ways to do that, including building a commemorative statue, dedicating a park, building a veterans' hospital, holding an annual celebration of veterans, initiating a scholarship fund, and founding a Reserve Officers' Training Corps (ROTC) program in the local schools.*

With the Generating cognitive process, the goal is to explore various hypotheses or ideas to address a novel or ill-defined problem. Often decisions or projects are based on quickly selecting one idea, without considering all the alternatives. Generating a novel solution might require examining the problem from another angle. Swartz & Parks (1994) comment, "Generative skills are creative thinking skills: They stretch our thinking and develop our imaginations" (p. 6). Pablo Picasso, an innovative artist, had a similar view: "Computers are useless. They can only give you answers." Creative ideas can lead to new paths.

In school, perhaps the problem is that the hallways are too crowded, causing numerous disciplinary incidents. The administration schedules more teachers to monitor the halls. However, perhaps the administration should consider other options, such as releasing classes at different times or teaching pro-social behaviors to students. Generating involves examining the problem from various angles. After understanding the various facets of the problem, flexible thinking is necessary to consider new ideas and different viewpoints, whereas close-minded thinking will limit the process. In this idea-generating stage, divergent thinking encourages ideas to emerge that are different from the current thinking about the problem, question, or idea. The ability to propose many solutions to problems is often termed "fluency." Earning 1,093 American patents, Thomas Edison said, "To have a great idea, have a lot of them." The ideas should also be varied (flexibility), unique (originality), and detailed (elaboration) (Swartz & Parks, 1994). Judgment is suspended until all possible options are generated. Some ideas might seem impractical, but it is important to collect a variety of novel ideas. Fogarty (1997) suggests the DOVE guidelines to assist with the generating process. "D" refers to students deferring judgment and considering all options. To consider different ideas, "O" represents opting for the outlandish. "V" stands for seeking a vast number of ideas, and "E" means to expand by connecting ideas to other ideas.

There are many instructional tasks on the Generating level, such as the following:

◆ **Social studies:** Students hypothesize about various ways in which the Civil War could have been averted.

◆ **Language arts:** Students rewrite the ending of a book by brainstorming possible endings or listing various modern-day adaptations to an older text.

◆ **Science:** Students create hypotheses explaining why the results of an experiment came out a certain way.

◆ **Math:** Students identify all the possible ways to solve a complex, real-world problem.

◆ **Vocational education:** Students examine all the different ways to launch an advertising campaign for a new technological device.

Another option is for students to record many different ways to solve a community problem. With each of these creative thinking tasks, they can be assessed according to criteria. For the book ending, teachers could assess if it represents the ideas of the text but in a modern-day adaptation. Due to the nature of this cognitive process, the assessment must be in an open-ended format.

Classroom Example Create Level: Generating
In-class instruction: Students research the role of economics in businesses.
Assessment: Over the years, the school lunch program has received reduced revenue due to fewer students buying lunches. Brainstorm all the possible reasons for this problem and ways to reverse this trend.

Create-Level Cognitive Process: Planning

The community group reviews possible options to honor local soldiers and considers the criteria: long-term impact, availability of financial resources, and the desire to show community support for the military. Based on these criteria, the group chooses to provide money to the local schools to support an ROTC that would also annually honor the local veterans in a commemorative ceremony. The group then creates a plan with four main steps:

1. *Contact the schools to discuss the prospect of starting an ROTC group.*

2. *If the schools support the idea, identify the financial resources needed to launch and maintain funding for the ROTC.*

3. *Begin fund-raising to obtain the needed financial resources to support the ROTC.*

4. *After the ROTC is established, collaborate yearly with it to plan a commemorative ceremony for veterans in the community.*

For each of the above items, group members are assigned tasks and completion dates are set.

Anderson and Krathwohl (2001) describe Planning as "devising a solution method that meets a problem's criteria, that is, developing a plan for solving the problem" (p. 87). This Planning process would involve identifying specific tasks to implement the action plan. This is a convergent phase in which the best idea from the Generating phase is selected and a plan of action is formed. First, the problem or issue is clearly identified, understood, and analyzed (Understand/Analyze level). Then, after brainstorming a list of good ideas (Generating), the best option is selected based on criteria (Critiquing). Paul and Elder (2005) states, "The mind when thinking well must simultaneously both produce and assess, both generate and judge, the products it constructs. Sound thinking requires both imagination and intellectual discipline" (p. 13). Finally, a plan is designed to implement the best solution (Planning). The Planning cognitive process is encouraged by the Partnership for 21st Century Skills (2011), which promotes students' using their creativity to make real contributions to the fields of study. Business leaders report that the competency upcoming leaders lack the most is strategic thinking, which hinges on critical thinking skills within the Planning cognitive process (Chartrand, Ishikawa, & Flander, 2009).

In English class, students can create an outline to plan their persuasive news article to address a community problem or use graphic organizers to help them organize their thoughts. This type of activity and the following are examples at the Planning level:

- Science: Students design a scientific experiment to test an idea.

- Math: Students develop a plan to address a complex, real-world math problem.

Sometimes in their planning, students will realize the solution is not correct and need to stop, reverse course, and switch to another idea. Often in open-ended problem-solving, there may be more than one correct plan for accomplishing a goal.

Classroom Example
Create Level: Planning

In-class instruction:

Students research the role of economics in businesses.

Assessment:

Based on the ideas you generated to increase the lunchroom revenue, select the best idea and design a plan for a marketing campaign to increase the percentage of students buying lunches in our school.

Create-Level Cognitive Process: Producing

Two members of the community group visit the principals of the local middle school and high school. The administrators are thrilled at the prospect of starting the ROTC, but register their concern for supporting the program due to limited financial resources. The community members assure the principals that the community would be financially supporting the group on a yearly basis. The principals agree to meet with the district office to discuss the initiative. After all parties agree to move forward, the group begins its fund-raising program. The appropriate ROTC officials are contacted to initiate the program. After about a year of planning, the new ROTC program is launched in the local schools. Local veterans are on hand to celebrate the new program as well as to be honored. A year later, the new ROTC students plan their first commemorative ceremony for local veterans.

Producing is the follow-through of the plan developed in the Planning cognitive process. In the Apply level, a student makes something new by following a procedure. At the Producing level, however, a student must analyze the information (Differentiating, Organizing, and Attributing), brainstorm possibilities to address the question (Generating), select the best option (Critiquing), design a plan to implement a solution (Planning), and then carry out the solution that is different entirely from the original sources (Producing). All these steps must be followed in a Producing-level task. Many times students "create" products like a brochure. However, they merely use the brochure to list facts on a given topic—a low-level task—rather than giving the brochure an authentic audience or purpose. By contrast, the Producing cognitive level requires complex and deep thinking.

Teachers and schools often conduct action research projects involving all three of the cognitive processes in the Create level by generating solutions to a school problem (Generating), creating an action plan (Planning), and implementing the plan (Producing). For instructional tasks, students can write a research paper, conduct an experiment, collect and analyze poll data, and draft a proposed bill for the state legislature. Authentic assessments provide ways to create instructional tasks and assessments at this cognitive level. For example, your school is going to start a school television show that will be broadcast to the community and students. Your class is assigned to design a news program. To do this well, extensive research and planning would be important. Researching other news programs and brainstorming ideas for the program (Generating) would prepare for the show. Then the group would prioritize goals for the program and design a plan for launching and maintaining the show (Planning). Finally, the group would begin producing the show (Producing). The benefit of authentic tasks like this is that they replicate the complexities, creativity, and collaboration required in the real world. They nurture skills that employers desire (Partnership for 21st Century Skills, 2011).

Classroom Example
Create Level: Producing

In-class instruction:

Students research the role of economics in businesses.

Assessment:

Students implement their marketing campaign plan to increase the percentage of students buying school lunches.

Inquiry and Problem-Solving

Inquiry and problem-solving lessons often address the cognitive processes within the Create level. Problem-solving refers to the step-by-step process of addressing a situation and determining a solution, often while encountering obstacles (Reed, 2000). This process involves generating options, planning a solution to solve the problem, decision-making, and then implementing a solution. One problem-solving model is called design thinking:

- ◆ **Identify an opportunity:** Identify a school or community issue and gather information about the problem.

- ◆ **Design:** Brainstorm solutions to the problems and research the best ideas.

- ◆ **Prototype:** Identify how the solution will work—sketch, build, make a prototype.

- ◆ **Get feedback:** Ask experts to review work and give feedback for improvement.

- ◆ **Scale and spread:** Plan the implementation, which might include work subgroups to accomplish the tasks.

- ◆ **Present:** Present the ideas in an authentic setting, whether via Skype or face to face (Ray, 2012).

These models provide ways for students to structure their thinking to design solutions. This model represents the cognitive processes within the Create level.

Critical thinking also is connected to a movement in education toward inquiry-based or problem-based learning. According to Schamel and Ayres (1992), students learn in a more effective manner when they generate their own questions based on their observations rather than developing a solution to a situation or problem with a predetermined answer. After students identify a question, they identify resources needed, including potential experts. In collaboration with the teacher, students establish the learning target for the project and the assessment. The teacher monitors progress through checking the completion timeline. The students' final project would be an authentic performance task. Many science teachers embrace the active, inquiry-based teaching model where students design a solution to a problem, requiring higher levels of cognition. While this model moves away from the rote memorization of scientific concepts, there is supporting evidence that students learn as many basic facts through this model as in a teacher-directed lecture. The positive benefit with this model is that students tend to be able to recall their learning for a longer time (Gabel & National Science Teachers Association, 1994).

Summary

For decades, Benjamin Bloom's cognitive taxonomy has been used by educators throughout the world to classify learning tasks. The recent revisions by Anderson and Krathwohl (2001) produced the six levels Remember, Understand, Apply, Analyze, Evaluate, and Create. Within each level are multiple cognitive processes to further describe the kind of thinking in each level. The levels and cognitive processes provide a frame of reference to examine lessons and assessments and determine the level of thinking expected.

Discuss

♦ Thinking back to your educational experience, what was one instructional task that enhanced your learning about a particular content area? What level on Bloom's taxonomy was the task?

♦ Describe the strategies used by teachers you had who *did* and who *did not* encourage you to think critically. At what level would you classify those strategies?

Take Action

1. Cognitive Domain Planning Tool

Using the Cognitive Domain Planning Tool (Figure 2.29), list the instructional strategies and formative and summative assessments for a unit of study.

♦ How much time do you spend teaching at each of the cognitive levels?

♦ Have you found a difference in student learning with the strategies that were taught on the higher levels?

♦ What low-level activity or assessment could you remove and what instructional task or assessment could you add to enhance the critical thinking skills in your unit?

2. Bloom's Taxonomy Question Starters

Using the chart labeled Bloom's Taxonomy Question Starters (Figure 2.30, pages 46–48), reflect on your questioning.

♦ Which question stems do you typically use?

♦ Which higher-level question stems could you start using?

♦ If you use higher-level questions, how does this affect wait time after questioning?

♦ If you gave your students this chart, how could they lead the questioning in your class?

♦ How could you use this chart to remind yourself to pose higher-level questions?

3. Bloom's Taxonomy Task Prompts

Using the chart labeled Bloom's Taxonomy Task Prompts (Figure 2.31, pages 49–50), examine the tasks at the various levels.

♦ Circle tasks and assessments you use in your instruction that are similar to the task prompts at each level.

♦ What are some suggested tasks at the Analyze, Evaluate, and Create levels that you could incorporate into your instruction?

Figure 2.29 **Cognitive Domain Planning Tool**

This tool allows you to examine your current instruction to determine how many of your instruction tasks and assessments for a particular unit are at which level. For a given unit of study, identify the instructional tasks, formative assessments, and summative assessments for each cognitive process.

Cognitive Domain Planning Tool			
Process Categories	Instructional Tasks	Formative Assessments	Summative Assessments
Remember			
1.1 Recognizing			
1.2 Recalling			
Understand			
2.1 Interpreting			
2.2 Exemplifying			
2.3 Classifying			
2.4 Summarizing			
2.5 Inferring			
2.6 Comparing			
2.7 Explaining			
Apply			
3.1 Executing			
3.2 Implementing			
Analyze			
4.1 Differentiating			
4.2 Organizing			
4.3 Attributing			
Evaluate			
5.1 Checking			
5.2 Critiquing			
Create			
6.1 Generating			
6.2 Planning			
6.3 Producing			

Figure 2.30   **Bloom's Taxonomy Question Starters**

Bloom's Taxonomy Question Starters	
Remembering	
Recognizing	Who, what, when, and where questions when students must select the answer ♦ For example, "Government by the people would describe which type of government—democracy or monarchy?"
Recalling	Who, what, when, and where questions when the student must recall the answer from memory ♦ For example, "Government by the people would describe which type of government?" ♦ Repeat back …
Understand	
Interpreting	♦ Can you say that in a different way? ♦ What does this mean? ♦ How would you describe _____ to another person? ♦ Define in your own words _____. ♦ Can you describe that picture?
Exemplifying	♦ What is another example of _____? ♦ What is an example of _____ in your life?
Classifying	♦ What is _____ an example of? ♦ How might you sort _____ into groups or categories? ♦ What rules or characteristics have been used to form the groups or categories?
Summarizing	♦ What is the main idea of the reading? ♦ Can you summarize what you just said? ♦ What is another title for this reading?
Inferring	♦ What are the implications of _____? ♦ Why did the author do _____? ♦ What can you conclude from the evidence or pieces of information? ♦ In this context, what was intended by saying/doing that? ♦ How is this connected to _____? ♦ What do you think will probably happen next? ♦ What is the relationship between _____ and _____?
Comparing	♦ How is _____ like _____? ♦ Why is _____ like _____? ♦ Can you distinguish between _____ and _____? ♦ How are _____ and _____ different? ♦ Describe the differences between _____ and _____.

(continued)

Bloom's Taxonomy Question Starters	
Explaining	◆ Based on the information so far, what will happen next? ◆ Predict the effects or implications of _____. ◆ Describe what might have caused this to happen. ◆ How would you change _____?
Apply	
Executing	◆ Using the taught procedure, how would you solve this problem? ◆ How can you use this procedure in some other instance?
Implementing	◆ Which procedure would you use to solve this problem? ◆ What is another way you could arrive at the solution?
Analyze	
Differentiating	◆ What information do you need to solve this problem or approach this task? ◆ Describe what facts in the informational source support _____. ◆ Which piece of evidence or information is most important to consider? ◆ What evidence have you got to back that up?
Organizing	◆ What familiar pattern do you notice? ◆ How could you organize or combine these ideas? ◆ How would you combine, or organize, _____ and _____?
Attributing	◆ Which is fact, opinion, or inference? ◆ What are the motives behind _____? ◆ What are the reasons for both perspectives? ◆ How would this look from the viewpoint of _____? ◆ What is the point of view of the author? ◆ What are the other viewpoints? ◆ What assumptions must we make to accept that conclusion? ◆ Should we accept these assumptions or question them? ◆ What are other ways of looking at this issue? ◆ Would you rather be _____ or _____? Why? ◆ Would you like to be _____? Why or why not? ◆ What is your opinion on _____? What evidence do you have to support your opinion?

(continued)

Bloom's Taxonomy Question Starters	
Evaluate	
Checking	◆ How could we verify that was true?
	◆ Is that always true?
	◆ Why do you believe that?
	◆ How strong are those arguments?
	◆ Is there a defect in any of the data or evidence provided?
	◆ How credible is that claim?
	◆ What are the reasons for the claim?
	◆ What is your basis for saying that?
	◆ Do the conclusions follow the reasoning?
	◆ How can we check to see if this argument is accurate?
	◆ What additional information do we need to resolve this question?
	◆ What are the strengths and weaknesses of this piece of evidence?
Critiquing	◆ Appraise, critique, judge, or evaluate _____. Support your appraisal, critique, judgment, or evaluation with evidence.
	◆ Why do you suppose that is good?
	◆ Is this _____ successful? What evidence do you have to support your opinion?
	◆ Could _____ be better? Why or why not?
	◆ Which is better? Why?
	◆ How would you rate or judge _____?
	◆ What choice would you have made? Support your position.
	◆ What are the arguments pro and con?
	◆ What are the advantages or disadvantages of _____?
	◆ Take a position on _____ and justify, support, defend, or prove your position.
	◆ Why do you think that was the right answer or solution?
	◆ Are there any undesirable consequences that we can and should foresee?
	◆ What are the consequences of doing things that way?
	◆ Explain what criteria you would use to evaluate which is the best option.
	◆ What is the most (least) important part?
	◆ How effective is _____?
Create	
Generating	◆ What are some alternatives to solving this problem that we haven't yet explored?
	◆ For this problem, what do you think would happen if _____ ? Why?
Planning	◆ What steps would you take to implement your plan?
Producing	◆ What product would best achieve the desired result?

Source: Some items adapted from Stanley (2006) and Stiggins, Arter, Chappuis, & Chappuis (2004).

Figure 2.31 **Bloom's Taxonomy Task Prompts**

Bloom's Taxonomy Task Prompts	
Remembering	
Recognizing	◆ Match the word and definition. ◆ Using a word bank, label a diagram.
Recalling	◆ Make a list of all the information you remember. ◆ Answer fact-based questions in a typical *Jeopardy* game.
Understand	
Interpreting	◆ Explain the concepts studied to a student who has never heard of this before. ◆ Make a list of the main ideas in the passage. ◆ Draw a picture or symbol to represent _____. ◆ Cut out pictures that represent _____. ◆ Create a hand motion to symbolize _____. ◆ In your own words, describe _____. ◆ Draw a cartoon showing the sequence of events.
Exemplifying	◆ Identify another example of _____. ◆ Explain how this information applies to your life. ◆ Provide an example of _____.
Classifying	◆ Group the key words into clusters of similar ideas. ◆ Classify the following _____ into categories.
Summarizing	◆ Write a news report summarizing _____. ◆ Create an outline of _____.
Inferring	◆ Create an analogy for _____. ◆ Create a metaphor for _____. ◆ Describe the relationship between _____ and _____. ◆ Identify ways in which one action could positive and negatively impact other variables.
Comparing	◆ Compare _____ and _____ based on the following elements: _____.
Explaining	◆ Create a cause-and-effect diagram. ◆ If _____ happens, what might happen? ◆ Explain how alternative actions might impact _____.
Apply	
Executing	◆ Determine the longitude and latitude of a city on a map. ◆ After learning to create a graph or table, design a table.
Implementing	◆ Write a letter of complaint to a company. ◆ After collecting survey data, select the best way to show the data.

(continued)

Bloom's Taxonomy Task Prompts	
Analyze	
Differentiating	◆ Mark out any irrelevant information in the problem or data set.
Organizing	◆ Create a way to organize the data in order to draw meaningful conclusions. ◆ Combine or organize the information in a meaningful way. ◆ Organize the information provided in appropriate categories. ◆ Put the information into a flowchart or a diagram. ◆ Create a chart or graph to show _____.
Attributing	◆ Identify the pros and cons of _____. ◆ Describe your own biases regarding this idea. ◆ Conduct a debate about an issue.
Evaluate	
Checking	◆ Examine the source and determine if it would be appropriate to support an argument. ◆ For the given source, identify the weaknesses and strengths. ◆ Review each source cited to determine the quality of information and evidence presented. ◆ Identify the claim and the supporting evidence. ◆ Highlight unsupported claims.
Critiquing	◆ Select the best option for the given problem or idea based on criteria (e.g., feasibility, consequences). ◆ Prioritize the solutions to the problem. ◆ Put in order of importance the key actions. ◆ Evaluate according to criteria the best _____. ◆ Identify the criteria to measure success. ◆ Determine the costs and benefits for each given solution. ◆ Evaluate a classmate's work based on rubric criteria. ◆ Determine the best course of action or decision based on a set of criteria.
Create	
Generating	◆ Create a list of all the possible solutions for _____ (a real-world problem). ◆ What would change if _____? ◆ Invent a solution for _____. ◆ Formulate a hypothesis for _____. ◆ Design a survey to _____.
Planning	◆ Create a plan to solve a problem over time. ◆ Draw up a plan to show how your idea will work.
Producing	◆ Deliver a presidential speech outlining a plan to address a real-world problem. ◆ Design a website to persuade your community to take action on an environmental issue.

Misconceptions, Challenges, and a Solution

*The world we have created is a product of our thinking;
it cannot be changed without changing our thinking.*
—Albert Einstein

"Critical thinking" is a term often used, but sometimes misunderstood, leading to many misconceptions among educators. Due to the misunderstanding about higher-level thinking, teachers sometimes use lower-level assessments and instructional tasks. However, there is a solution! By using interpretive exercises, teachers can design instructional tasks and assessments at higher levels of cognitive complexity. This chapter will address critical thinking misconceptions, consider the challenges infusing cognitively engaging tasks and assessments, and then present a solution.

Misconceptions

Misconceptions about Bloom's cognitive taxonomy are rampant. Eleven misconceptions will be addressed here. Due to these confusions, many teachers believe they are providing critical-thinking tasks when, in reality, they are not. By recognizing these common misunderstandings, teachers can plan more appropriate instructional tasks and assessments for their students.

#1: Critical Thinking Assessments Used Multiple Times

As an administrator, I had my staff work together to revise assessments. After working with the teachers in one content area to get their summative assessment revised, I was thrilled that their work incorporated deep-thinking processes. The day before the test, I was doing some routine walk-through visits in the classrooms. I noticed one of the teachers had the test in hand and was asking the test questions to prepare students for the next day's assessment. The class then discussed the answers to the high-level questions. As I returned to my office, I realized that I had not clearly communicated what critical thinking meant. The questions the teacher asked on the review day were high-level. However, if the teacher used those same questions the next day, then students would just be remembering the answers and not thinking critically, because they would already know the answers due to the previous day's discussion.

While I was conducting training for another school, a school counselor had an epiphany and said, "So you mean that we really don't know if the test is high-level simply by looking at the questions." She was correct. The items on the test might be high-level, but if the teacher has already discussed the items in class before the test, then the test would represent the lowest level on Bloom's taxonomy, the Remember level. Once the answer to a high-level question is discussed, the assessment item functions as a memorized answer for future testing purposes. After the answers to a critical-thinking question have been discussed, different questions have to be constructed for further assessments in order to maintain the high level of cognitive complexity.

#2: Teachers Using High-Level Bloom's Words

In your desperation for help in understanding Bloom's work, have you searched the Internet and located verbs that align to each level? Or have you purchased a Bloom's flip chart to help you? I affectionately call these people "Bloom's Flip Chart Addicts." While the flip charts and verb charts can be helpful resources, teachers who do not understand Bloom's framework select a word from one of the higher levels of Bloom's framework and simply plunk it into an instructional objective or assessment—for example, "Synthesize the passage and explain who is the main character." Using a high-level verb like "synthesize" does not mean the question automatically becomes a high-level assessment item. Consider what level of thinking is being requested. In this case, the student is most likely identifying the main character; if it is a new passage, then it would be on an Understand level.

Due to this confusion, I recommend using the lists of verbs for each Bloom's level carefully, if at all. The word "explain" can be used appropriately on several different levels of Bloom's taxonomy. For example, "Explain in your own words the definition of a *chemical solution*" is an Understand-level task, whereas "Explain what is the best solution for solving the recycling problem in our neighborhood" could be on the Create level. Many teachers misunderstand these lists, so I rarely use them. Instead, one strategy I recommend for teachers is examining the response time for students. Most of the time, low-level questions can be responded to quickly by students, whereas tasks or questions at the Analyzing level and above are almost impossible to answer orally. The complexity of Analyze-, Evaluate-, and Create-level tasks requires students to read the question several times, often put thoughts on paper, and perhaps even do some research before deriving a solution.

#3: Difficult Tasks Are High-Level Thinking Tasks

I am terrible at the game Trivial Pursuit. I depend on technology to help me remember trivia information. All the questions in *Trivial Pursuit* and *Jeopardy* games are low-level questions, on the Remember level, but they would be considered difficult. For example, to name a river in South Africa that you heard on television once, without the use of any resources, would be a difficult question for most people, but it is a fact and does not require higher-level thinking processes. Perhaps you know people who have a phenomenal memory but lack the ability to think critically. When selecting instructional tasks and assessments, teachers need to assess at what level on Bloom's taxonomy students will process the information. The level of difficulty and the level of thinking processes are different entities.

#4: Lessons Focus on Technology or Creative Arts Instead of the Thinking Levels of the Content

Teachers often incorporate technology or art into their assessments. When this happens, the assessment is often measuring two elements: technology use or creative arts *and* content. For example, a first-year teacher gave me a lesson plan with the objective, "Students will be able to create a PowerPoint presentation on George Washington." The teacher felt that this was on the Create level of Bloom's taxonomy. When we met before the lesson, I asked her what exactly students would be doing when they designed the presentation. She said that students would be looking up information online about Washington and summarizing the key events of his administration. In examining students' thinking about the social studies content, her assessment fit more on the Understanding level because they were summarizing. She also had a secondary purpose to utilize the technology. In this case, because students had already designed PowerPoint presentations before, they were applying that skill to this assignment. Therefore, the technology objective for this task would be classified on the Apply level, whereas the social studies content was on the Understanding level. This discrepancy often happens with creative art tasks like designing a mural or dramatic skit.

Most assessments are classified in regard to thinking using the content, unless of course the class focus is on technology use or creative arts. Consider students' use of technology and artistic skills as separate dimensions when assessing. Also, remember that the Bloom's level for the technology or creative art task may be on a different cognitive level than the thinking about the content in the task. Keep your focus on the content!

#5: Teachers Believe the Level of Thinking Is the Same for All Students

A teacher might design an assignment on one of the higher levels of Bloom's taxonomy and yet still have students turn in work at various levels on the taxonomy. For example, if the assignment was to create a storybook for elementary students about an environmental issue in the community, some students would design an original story and characters about a real community issue. However, other students might struggle and produce a story that mimics one they had read earlier. Thus, the task was on a high level, but the work produced was on various levels: the students who created the novel story would be working at the Create level, whereas those who imitated a story already written would be on a much lower level.

#6: Student Thinking Is Best Assessed Through Oral Questioning

When I was conducting a school training, the teachers explained that the district office the next day would be conducting walk-through observations in the school looking for higher-level thinking instruction. The teachers were told that the observers would be recording only what was said by the teacher. I commented to the principal that this would not give a fair picture of the level of thinking in the school because often the highest levels of thinking are assessed by assignments and tasks with details recorded on paper or technology. With higher levels of cognitive processing, students need time to think. In fact, students might work several days or more to produce a product at the Create level.

#7: Multiple-Choice Assessments Demand Low Level Thinking; Writing Tasks Require High-Level Thinking

Assessment formats can also bridge across several Bloom's levels. Another misconception is that multiple-choice questions can assess only basic knowledge. Multiple-choice questions can assess understandings on the Remember, Understand, Apply, and Analyze levels. For example, high-level thinking multiple-choice questions can ask students to identify the best conclusion from a data set. Many testing companies use multiple-choice questions to assess students' higher-level thinking due to the ability to efficiently score student responses.

Some teachers think that a question that requires an open-ended response is automatically a higher-level item. However, some essay prompts simply require students to produce facts. Writing can be a lower-level task if it does not call forth new ideas or ideas organized in a new way. Thus, it is important to examine the open-ended response prompt to ensure it requires higher levels of thinking. If the teacher wants to assess lower levels of thinking, a selected-response assessment format provides a quick and efficient way to assess this knowledge. Since open-ended questions are time-consuming to score, teachers should reserve open-ended questions to address the higher levels of thinking in Bloom's taxonomy. For example, "Which political candidate is the best choice for our state? Why?"

#8: Bloom's Tasks Do Not Match Standards or Student Needs

While Bloom's taxonomy defines the levels, the point is to increase the level of thinking. Sometimes educators disagree about at what level to categorize the instructional task or assessment. Essentially, teachers should focus on developing higher-level instructional experiences and not spend time arguing about the Bloom's levels for tasks and assessments.

With the pressure incorporated in higher-level processes, sometimes teachers select a Bloom's level to work toward which might not be a good fit with the standard they are teaching. For example, a teacher is teaching a new skill: how to add fractions. To incorporate higher-level thinking, the teacher determines that instruction will be on the Create level. However, to learn the skill, students really need practice at the Apply level. After the skill is mastered, it might be appropriate for students to propose, design, and implement a Create-level task.

It is not necessary to teach and assess at the highest level of Bloom's taxonomy, the Create level, in order to attain every content standard. Create-level tasks often require a significant amount of time for students to complete. Given the numerous standards expected to be taught, it probably is not possible to have a Create-level task for each concept. However, Create-level tasks can be selectively planned and show a culminating performance of students' knowledge and abilities.

When deciding at what level to teach to, teachers should ascertain the students' background knowledge. It is important that teachers build on the students' prior knowledge. If students already have a strong understanding of the content, challenging students to Analyze, Evaluate, or Create would stretch their thinking. However, some classes may feel overwhelmed when assigned a Create-level task. Having students regularly develop their thinking on Analyze- and Evaluate-level tasks can build up their skills, preparing them to complete a Create-level task.

Some subjects seem to lend themselves easily to the higher levels. For example, in language arts classes, students do quite a bit of original writing that is on the Create level. Other classes are heavily embedded with skills to teach; in math, for example, quite a bit of instruction is on the Apply level.

#9: Young Students Cannot Complete Higher-Level Tasks

Some consider that higher-level thinking tasks are appropriate only for high-school and college students. However, high-level thinking tasks are suitable for all ages. In fact, if students in primary grades do not master cognitive skills like comparing, classifying, sequencing, and predicting, students rarely achieve grade-level performance in reading comprehension and independent learning (Siegler, 1998). Therefore, young students need to be taught thinking skills in order for them to successfully understand content.

#10: Some Educators Have False Assumptions on How Students Learn

Paul & Elder (2007) state that some teachers design lessons based on false assumptions, including the following:

1. Lecture content can be absorbed with minimal intellectual engagement on the part of the students.

2. Students can learn important content without much intellectual work.

3. Memorization is the key to learning, so that students need to store up lots of information (that they can use later when they need it).

If instruction predominantly consists of students memorizing information, they will forget a large amount of their learning. In research measuring student thinking, teachers whose lessons centered on teaching facts or specific problem types for a test had students who did not develop deep conceptual understandings or were unable to apply their learning to different circumstances (Shepard, Hammerness, Darling-Hammond, & Rust, 2005). When students engage in deep processing of content, it leads to greater transfer of the knowledge into long-term memory and content mastery. Paul and Elder (2007) state, "The only capacity we can use to learn is human thinking. If we think well while learning, we learn well. If we think poorly while learning, we learn poorly" (p. 8). Thus, in order to learn in any content area, students must think critically by evaluating and analyzing the content in that discipline. By thinking at a deep level, students learn to internalize the content and make it meaningful to them. By structuring learning experiences around high-level thinking and content engagement, teachers help their students become knowledge producers instead of simply knowledge consumers. According to Paul and Elder (2007),

> Educated persons function differently from uneducated persons. They are able to enter and intellectually empathize with alternate ways of looking at things. They change their minds when evidence or reasoning require it. They are able to internalize important concepts within a discipline and inter-relate those concepts with other important concepts both within and

among disciplines. They are able to reason well to think their way through complex problems. If students are to become educated persons, teachers must place thinking at the heart of the curriculum; they must require students to actively work ideas into their thinking using their thinking. (p. 9)

In essence, deep thinking is inseparable from life-long learning.

#11: High-Level Tasks Are for Gifted Students

Sometimes teachers will document on their lesson plan that gifted students will receive higher-order thinking questions as an adaptation. On the other end of the spectrum, learners who seem to be less capable are given fill-in-the-blank worksheets requiring only low levels of thinking. Unless all students gain access to cognitively engaging tasks, the achievement gap will continue to widen (Torff, 2011). President Barack Obama has stated that every student will graduate from high school ready for college and a career (U.S. Department of Education, 2010). For this to happen, all students must be exposed to critical thinking tasks.

However, not all students get equal access to critical thinking tasks. Not surprisingly, a more significant focus on high-level critical thinking activities has been found in upper-track classes (Raudenbush, Rowan, & Cheong, 1993). Teachers in minority schools often support reducing the availability of critical thinking tasks for disadvantaged students (Torff, 2005, 2006, 2008). These teachers have good intentions, believing that the higher-level tasks will frustrate students. However, evidence shows that disadvantaged students along with advantaged students benefit from cognitively engaging curriculum (Zohar & Dori, 2003; Pogrow, 1990, 1994). Schools can harm students by underestimating their abilities. When students come to schools with different skills and cultural experiences, schools notice these differences and assume the students are incapable of cognitively complex tasks, instead of having a growth mind-set and seeing all students as having potential to learn (Dweck, 2007; Olson, 2009). Student potential should be viewed as an iceberg, with most of the children's aptitudes concealed from view (Tomlinson & Javius, 2012). With a supportive environment and high expectations, these abilities will be revealed. If disadvantaged students are deprived of cognitively complex tasks, they will fall further behind in a repetitive cycle.

If all students are to reach high levels of learning, then we cannot continue to provide critical-thinking activities just to our advanced students. In our democracy, schools are charged with providing a quality education to all students. If we fail to offer opportunities for all students to engage in complex thinking opportunities, we fail to equip them with the tools to be successful. Critical-thinking activities help all students to develop deeper understandings of concepts (Paul & Elder, 2007).

Moore and Stanley (2010) compare thinking to sports. Any person can learn to be better at critical thinking if given enough time and practice. When students initially work on critical-thinking tasks, they need modeling and practice, just as with any other skill students learn. They need to be coached on strategies to approach the task and given graphic organizers to construct their thoughts. Without such support, students may become overwhelmed. Teachers should not get frustrated if at first students do not receive high marks on cognitively complex assignments. Practice and feedback will improve students' abilities. We all have seen teachers who required students to produce work that engaged higher-level thinking skills. Those teachers raised the level of expectations, modeled thinking strategies, provided many developmentally appropriate opportunities for students to practice their thinking skills, offered encouragement and constructive feedback, and found students could reach high levels of thinking.

Challenges

The need for embedding critical thinking tasks into the curriculum is clear. However, there are several challenges to increasing the quantity of critical thinking tasks in classrooms. Through awareness of these challenges, educators can be prepared for obstacles they may encounter as they try to implement a cognitively complex curriculum.

Familiarity and Comfort with Low-Level Tasks and Assessments

Often, teachers create assessments at a Remembering level, the lowest level of thinking in Bloom's taxonomy. In a research study of more than 8,800 test questions created by teachers representing elementary through high school tests, Fleming and Chambers (1983) found that nearly 80 percent were at the Remember level. Almost ten years later, a national representative survey found similar results. Through content analysis, Madaus, West, Harmon, Lomax, & Viator (1992) determined that only 3 percent of assessment items on tests represented high-level conceptual knowledge and only about 5 percent of the total items sampled assessed higher-level thinking skills of any type. The other 95 percent of items sampled involved the low-level skills of recalling information, calculating, and using formulas to solve routine problems similar to problems worked in the textbook or in class. These results are echoed by Goodlad (2004), who reported that 90 percent of the time in schools, teachers relayed information to students from a textbook and then assessed them on their memorization of this information.

With a large portion of teacher-designed tests assessing at a low level, students may think that education is more about memorizing facts than thinking deeply to develop conceptual understandings. Since students typically perform better on low-level thinking items, teachers may presume that their students are more capable than they are because students were not expected to think at high levels. However, when students are called upon to use high-level processes on state and national assessments, those who have not regularly employed these thinking skills will be unprepared.

As a new principal, I was aware that my school's math scores were relatively low in comparison to the scores in other academic areas. I observed one teacher and noticed that students were completing all the formula-type questions, which were on the Apply level using the Executing cognitive process. Students were not using the math skills in the kind of real-world word problems that were included on the state assessment. This misalignment was causing our students to be unprepared for the state assessment. The math teachers collaboratively revised their assessments and instructional tasks to include more real-world problems that required critical thinking and problem-solving. Their hard work over the course of three years led to a 32 percent increase on the state assessment scores. To prepare students appropriately for state assessments as well as life, teachers must develop classroom assessments with high levels of cognitive complexity.

Lack of Understanding of Bloom's Taxonomy

The honest fact is that teachers struggle to create assessment items because they lack the necessary understanding of Bloom's taxonomy and the strategies to increase the critical-thinking level of assessments. During their undergraduate years, education majors face a wealth of information that must be learned, from classroom management to lesson planning. Designing high-level assessments is often taught, but might not be considered the most critical part of an undergraduate teacher candidate's program. During their first years as a teacher, in professional learning communities and through professional development, beginning teachers might receive additional training to refine their skills in developing high-level tasks and assessments. However, because many teachers still feel unsure about their assessment-designing skills, they rely on textbook questions or other assessment item banks which may or may not provide cognitively complex assessments.

With the thorough descriptions in this book of the Bloom's levels and the examples in subsequent chapters, the hope is you will be able to identify the different levels of thinking and design instructional tasks and assessments that require students to use their critical-thinking skills.

More Time

Unfortunately, assessment items with high cognitive demand take a long time to create. The process is much longer than for low-level questions as teachers must create new situations in which students can apply their knowledge. In addition, it takes students longer to answer cognitively complex assessment items because more thinking and processing time is required. Teachers who incorporate higher-level assessments often reduce the number of items on the tests because of the time it takes for students to answer questions.

To mitigate this difficulty, teachers can incorporate interpretive items into their assessments. Interpretative items are a way to increase the level of cognitive complexity of the instructional tasks and assessments by incorporating graphics, scenarios, and quotes.

A Solution: Interpretive Exercises

As educators search for ways to increase the level of thinking in their instructional tasks and assessments to meet the demands of the Common Core State Standards for students to engage in high-level thinking skills, one approach is through embedding interpretive exercises. Nitko and Brookhart (2007) defines interpretive exercises as "items or assessment tasks that require the student to use reading material, graphs, tables, pictures, or other material to answer the items" (p. 514). Interpretive exercises begin with introductory materials like graphics, quotes, or scenarios. Students then are asked to examine the introductory materials and use them to complete the instructional task or assessment. In the interpretive exercise example below, a scenario is provided about a candidate wanting to run for the U.S. presidency. In order for students to complete this assessment, they would need to know the qualifications for running for the presidency and then scrutinize the scenario provided to determine which of the answer choices is correct.

Figure 3.1 **Interpretive Exercise Example**

Susan May is running for president. She is a forty-year-old teacher from Dallas, Texas. Susan has lived in Texas for the past twenty years but was born and raised in Paris, France. Her parents are French citizens. At the age of twenty she moved to attend the Texas A&M University. While in Texas, she became an American citizen. Based only on the information provided, what would prevent Susan from being eligible to run for president at this point in her life?

a. Susan is a woman.

b. Susan is forty years old.

c. Susan has not lived in the United States her whole life.

d. Susan was not born a U.S. citizen.

e. None of the above

Interpretive exercises are most often incorporated into forced-choice assessments like multiple-choice questions or an extended response like short answers or essays. In some cases, the interpretive exercises can be the stimulus for students to create projects or products. The many advantages of interpretive exercises are discussed below. In subsequent chapters, numerous examples will be provided in a variety of assessment formats and subject areas.

Assessing Higher-Level Thinking Skills

Interpretive exercises provide numerous advantages; however, the main benefit is that they access higher cognitive levels. In such an exercise, as discussed before, students must encounter a novel problem or situation that requires them to assess the situation and derive an acceptable solution by using both their knowledge of the relevant subject matter and their reasoning skills. By using interpretive materials like graphs, pictures, or reading passages that students have not viewed previously, students are assessed at a higher cognitive level on the new task (Gronlund, 1981; Mehrens & Lehmann, 1984; Nitko 1983).

To answer an interpretive exercise, first students must understand the interpretive materials. Second, students must understand the question or task. They must then identify and access the background information that can help interpret the new materials. Students must make connections between introductory materials provided and their prior knowledge, which might include facts and terms to answer the question. Finally, students will complete the task, such as identifying the best hypothesis for the data provided, identifying the most important element in a piece of writing that needs to be revised, or evaluating which historical photograph best represents the time period.

Using interpretive materials can assess complex thinking skills such as reading ability, comprehension, mathematical thinking, problem-solving, writing skills, and graph and table interpretation (Haladyna, Downing, & Rodriguez, 2002; Hale & Astolfi, 2011). Interpretive exercises can also assess skills such as recognizing assumptions, identifying valid conclusions, interpreting relationships, differentiating between relevant and irrelevant information, and drawing inferences from reading (Hale & Astolfi, 2011). These exercises provide situations for students to employ their problem-solving skills as they identify problems; select which principles, generalizations, or criteria are relevant to interpreting the information; and utilize critical-thinking skills to answer the question. Haladyna, Downing, & Rodriguez (2002) note that interpretive materials are often used in large-scale assessments primarily due to their ability to capture students' thinking processes with great fidelity.

Establishing a Frame of Reference

Students come to assessment experiences with a variety of prior knowledge and experience. An assessment item that uses interpretive materials provides the necessary background information, making it a fair assessment (Hale & Astolfi, 2011).

Including Multistep Questions

In interpretive exercises, several questions can be based on the same introductory material. Often a series of assessment items based on introductory material can tap greater skills depth and breadth (Hale & Astolfi, 2011; Wainer & Kiely, 1987). Gronlund (2006) agrees: "Complex learning outcomes can frequently be more effectively measured by basing a series of test items on a common selection of introductory material" (p. 103). If the introductory material for an interpretive exercise includes several documents or a data set, several questions or tasks could be crafted to assess several concepts or skills or even varying levels of abilities.

Scoring and Reliability

Another benefit of interpretive exercises is that they can be paired with selected-response questions. Multiple-choice questions have gained a negative reputation as being capable only of assessing factual recall (e.g., vocabulary). However, well-written multiple-choice questions have the potential to assess higher-level thinking skills. Interpretive exercises paired with multiple-choice questions are a more efficient way to assess high-level skills compared to performance assessment. In less time, teachers can assess students' conceptual understanding about a broad range of topics. Such exercises can also be quickly scored due to the possibility of using a selected-response format. And unlike open-ended questions, these items can be objectively scored (Suskie, 2009).

Increasing Student Interest

Often students who have no idea how to answer a question will give up immediately. With interpretative materials, these students have something to examine and spur their thinking. The introductory information with text or graphics gives students something to initially spark their thinking. Additionally, interpretive materials can simulate real-world experiences as they ask students to analyze passages, draw conclusions from data charts, or examine a political cartoon. These applications of knowledge are more interesting than simply recalling information students have been told to memorize.

Aligning to Standards

In some cases it is nearly impossible to align to a standard without using interpretive materials. For example, if students are expected to apply their knowledge of math principles in real-world situations, then students must encounter a real-world situation. In English, to analyze the setting of text, students would need to read a passage from a new text to evaluate it. To determine if students can read a map, students need a map to analyze.

Simulating State and National Assessment Questions

Finally, these types of interpretive questions exist on state and national assessments. Using interpretive materials in class prepares students for the state and national assessments. For example, in 2011, Kentucky launched a new state assessment, Kentucky Performance Rating for Educational Progress (K-PREP). Samples of assessment items for the norm-referenced portion of the test were released. In this document there are multiple examples of interpretive exercises incorporating graphics, scenarios, and passages (Kentucky Department of Education, 2011).

Summary

Despite the misconceptions and challenges, there are many ways to include critical thinking in tasks and assessments. Interpretive materials provide a way to infuse critical-thinking skills into the curriculum. Exercises using graphics, scenarios, and quotes can help teachers meet the challenge of creating high-level tasks and assessments. Interpretive materials require students to utilize their higher-level thinking skills. The use of such exercises in class prepares students for state and national assessments, which already embed interpretive materials into their assessments. The next three chapters will explain various types of interpretive exercises using visuals, quotes, and scenarios while providing numerous examples of instructional tasks and assessments from a variety of content areas.

Discuss

- ◆ Which of the misconceptions in this chapter did you believe?
- ◆ Now that you have learned about the misconceptions, what changes do you need to make in your current practices?
- ◆ What are other misconceptions about cognitive complexity?
- ◆ How are schools perpetuating these misconceptions?

◆ Where have you seen interpretive exercises?

◆ How do you think interpretive exercises can help you in your classroom?

Take Action

◆ Review your instructional tasks and assessments. Do you currently use interpretive exercises?

◆ Search the Internet or company testing materials. What are some examples of interpretive materials?

Scenarios and Real-World Applications

One cannot be a good learner and a poor thinker.
—Richard Paul and Linda Elder

One way to create interpretive exercises is through the use of scenarios and real-world applications of students' knowledge. By including new introductory materials, tasks and assessments will move beyond the Remember level on Bloom's taxonomy to increasing levels of cognitive complexity. Scenarios, real-world examples, and authentic tasks are a way to infuse deep cognitive thinking into lessons and assessments in an engaging context.

This chapter will describe how using scenarios, real-world examples, and authentic tasks can increase high-level thinking. Suggestions for constructing instructional tasks and assessments using such interpretive items are identified, followed by examples from several content areas.

Types of Real-World Applications

This chapter presents three ways to incorporate interpretive exercises into lessons and assessments: scenarios, real-world examples, and authentic tasks. A description and the benefits of each are included in this section.

Scenarios

A scenario is a sequence of events or a fictional description of an action or events. Scenarios provide a way of assessing students' application of knowledge in a simulated context. Scenarios are already used in many professional arenas to assess knowledge. Students studying to be nurses read situations or case studies and decide on the best course of action. In law schools, future lawyers identify the issues at stake in a scenario and determine the best way to proceed in the given situation. Perhaps even in your undergraduate teacher education program or state licensure test you were presented with classroom management situations and asked to determine the best way to handle the situation. A scenario example for a Spanish I class is provided below.

> The nurse asks a patient what is wrong. Which answer below might be something the patient would say?
>
> **a. Me duele la cabeza.**
>
> b. Me siento feliz.
>
> c. Me duele me lapis.
>
> d. Me siento sola.

In this scenario, the first choice translated means, "My head hurts." For this example, students must be able not only to translate the statements, but also to identify which one appropriately applies to the situation.

When simulations are too expensive or too time-consuming, scenarios provide an easier way to assess thinking in a similar context while maintaining higher-level thinking. Scenarios are thus often used on state and national assessments. The Programme for International Student Assessment (PISA) measured 15-year-old students' ability to apply math and science concepts in real-world scenarios. In these assessments, U.S. students were among the lowest performers (Lemke et al. 2004). If teachers embed scenarios into their instruction and assessments, students will be better prepared to apply their knowledge on state and national assessments. For classroom instruction and assessments, scenarios can be complex, like a case study with lots of information to comprehend and analyze, or less complicated, like the Spanish example.

Real-World Examples

Real-world examples move beyond the simulated context to provide direct connections between the content and authentic situations. Through real-world instances, students become aware of the extension of their learning in realistic circumstances. In the world and history are examples of concepts that align to content in the curriculum. Unlike fictional scenarios, real-world examples are actual instances that provide a way for students to see the content applied in a meaningful, real way. Real-world situations provide a perfect opportunity for teachers to showcase how student learning applies to contexts outside of school. Additionally, real examples from the students' local community and those that relate to their interests can pique student attention in the topic studied. Below is a real-world example for a business or social studies class.

In 2007, Apple sold around 1 million iPhones. In 2011, around 71 million iPhones were sold.

A. Describe the different marketing techniques Apple is using compared to other companies to increase sales.

B. If Apple wants to continue to be successful, what are two marketing changes that must be made within the next ten years?

In this example, students use their knowledge of marketing to analyze and suggest changes to marketing techniques. As shown in this situation, real-world situations can appeal to students' interest.

Authentic Tasks

Another way to incorporate relevant learning experiences is through designing authentic tasks. While real-world examples connect to historical or current-day applications of the content, authentic tasks simulate job challenges, requiring research and multiple steps to create the solution or product. The Partnership for 21st Century Skills (2011) states,

> As educators pursue CCSS (Common Core State Standards) alignment, then, it is crucial to design curricula and assessment systems that emphasize authentic real-world problems, engage students in inquiry and exploration and provide opportunities for students to apply what they know in meaningful ways. (p. 10)

Authentic tasks align to 21st-century skills supporting student-centered approaches with problem-based learning and project-based learning. Through these experiences, students learn to collaborate while working on authentic problems that often positively impact the community (Rotherham & Willingham, 2009). Local business and community partners are a rich source of real-world problems that can be incorporated into an authentic task. Whether the issue is increasing the level of recycling, helping the police to stop graffiti, or designing a web page for a local business, students can devise ways to address the problem and propose realistic solutions. Students will be more motivated to engage in the task due to the real-world context. In addition, students can learn important skills to transfer to various careers, addressing the emphasis in the Common Core State Standards on college and career readiness.

When I was an administrator, my school's writing scores were low. The teachers were diligently working to improve students' writing abilities. I knew that I needed to do more to support the program, so I proposed starting an editorial board. Students who were good writers were selected to serve on this board. I told the student group that our main goal was to encourage student writing. When the editorial board met, the members read submissions by their peers, evaluating them based on the qualities of good writing. The board then selected a piece of writing to profile each week. The selected authors were acknowledged on the school's public address system, and their writing was showcased in our front hall. Visitors enjoyed reading their writing, and the students loved the attention. During editorial board meetings, I was amazed at the conversations among members as they critiqued the submitted work. They brought up points about focus, voice, and grammar. These students serving on the editorial board were doing a real-world job. With authentic tasks, the role of the students shifts from a passive role to assuming a real-world role such as a historian, sports analyst, scientist, or literary critic.

Authentic tasks also provide a way for students to demonstrate their learning in a more appropriate context for some standards. For example, if students are expected to develop persuasive writing, a multiple-choice test cannot appropriately assess this skill. If the goal of a technology class is for students to create technology products, again, multiple-choice assessments or essays would not align to the learning target. Another benefit of authentic tasks is that they can access the highest level on Bloom's taxonomy, the Create level. As students brainstorm solutions (Planning cognitive dimension), design a plan of action (Designing cognitive dimension), and implement their plan (Producing cognitive dimension), they are working at the highest cognitive levels. Selected-response questions cannot assess thinking on the Create level.

When designing an authentic task, teachers should first identify a role that is related to the intended learning target. Then, they need to identify the task, the product the students would produce, and the audience who would be interested in the product (see Figure 4.1).

Below are examples of authentic tasks in science, social studies, language arts, and math.

- ◆ Science: Acting as water conservationists (role), investigate ways to reduce water consumption in our school and propose an inexpensive and effective way to do so (task) in a presentation (product) to the principal (audience).

Figure 4.1 Designing an Authentic Task

1. **Real-world role:** What job will the students be simulating?

2. **Task:** What is the task that the students will complete?

3. **Product:** What type of product will students construct? Could students create different products, allowing for student choice?

4. **Audience:** Who will view the product? Is there someone beyond the classroom that would be interested in this work?

- **Social studies:** Acting as legislators, write a class constitution that identifies student rights, responsibilities, and duties as well as how the power will be distributed. This document will be used throughout the year to govern the classroom.

- **Language arts:** As an employee of a publishing company, select one book that was published fifty or more years ago by your company but is not widely known and would be appealing to the young adult market today. Prepare a persuasive presentation to convince the president of the publishing company to select your book for a new advertising campaign.

- **Math:** Hired as a Women's National Basketball Association recruiter, review the statistics on six prospects for this year's draft and select one basketball player that you would recruit. Based on statistics alone, prepare a persuasive report to convince your boss that this player is the best recruit for your team. (This example could be changed to other sports depending on students' interests.)

Higher-Level Thinking

Scenarios, real-world examples, and authentic tasks all provide an opportunity for students to think at higher levels, assuming that the task or assessment is different from those they have previously encountered. There are many ways to infuse scenarios, real-world examples, and authentic tasks with critical thinking. One way is to include both relevant and irrelevant information in the task, thus requiring students to first identify the salient information before completing the task. For example, for the Apple marketing question mentioned previously, students might need to do research prior to answering the question. During the research process, students would need to identify information pertinent to answering the question.

Another way to assess student thinking is by asking students to identify examples of concepts in scenarios or real-world examples. In a social studies assessment about the way a coach leads a team, students could identify, based on the details in the scenario, what type of government (e.g., democracy, dictatorship, oligarchy) the coach most clearly represented. In science, an assessment could describe a girl drinking a cold beverage on a hot day and noticing the water beads on the outside of the glass. Students then must identify which concept is represented by the water beads (condensation).

Scenarios, real-world examples, and authentic tasks can also include complex situations requiring problem-solving. First, students must understand the situation by diagnosing and interpreting the nature and root causes of the problem. Students can identify possible solutions and evaluate each. Finally, students would develop and implement a plan.

Often in scenarios and real-world examples common misconceptions will be included, challenging students to identify the mistake. In math and science this is often termed "error analysis." After identifying the error, students can correct the mistake. In scenarios and real-world situations, students could also identify assumptions made in the situation and propose alternative interpretations.

While problem-solving is often used in math, other content areas can include problem-solving tasks with real dilemmas students must address. For example, a local gym has been unable to increase its membership. Students should determine the best way advertising can be used to increase the gym's membership. This would be an example of an authentic task as students determine a solution to a problem.

Another way to engage students in higher-level thinking is through decision-making tasks. Through decision-making, students evaluate alternatives by using developed criteria and then select the best course of action. For example, students can examine a country's postwar statistics and determine the country's next best foreign policy action. This exercise requires students to evaluate complex information and consider the economic, social, environmental, and/or religious ramifications of their decision. Often in decision-making, complex issues must be examined along with divergent points of view.

Design Tips

When utilizing scenarios or real-world examples for instructional tasks or assessments, teachers should consider the following items:

◆ Select the standard first. Always start by identifying the learning target or standard that will be the focus for your instructional task or assessment.

◆ Consider including relevant and irrelevant information so students learn to review information critically and select information appropriate to the task.

◆ Whenever possible, relate the scenarios, examples, or tasks to students' interests.

◆ Make sure the task matches the skill level of the students.

◆ Be sure the scenario does not provide trigger words that give away the answer. For example, if the question is about a concept and includes some of the typical words in the definition, they can cause students to automatically select the correct answer without thinking deeply.

◆ Decide on the assessment format. Scenarios and real-world examples could be structured in a multiple-choice or open-ended format. The end product of an authentic assessment could be in a variety of formats, including a presentation, a web page, or a piece of writing.

In Figure 4.2, steps for designing these types of items are enumerated.

Figure 4.2 **Steps to Design**

1. Identify the learning target or standard.
2. Search for real-world examples, create your own scenario, or design the authentic task.
3. Check the task or assessment to ensure it requires higher-level thinking processes.
   - Verify that the question requires students to understand introductory materials before answering the question.
   - Check to ensure that the scenario is new to the students.
   - Confirm that the answer is not directly in the introductory materials and that students must make connections to prior knowledge taught in the class. If the assessment is measuring students' conceptual understanding, be careful not to use terms that would make students automatically connect the question to an answer.
4. Determine if the assessment item is appropriate for the students' knowledge and skill level.
5. Ensure that the task or assessment contains all the information needed to answer the item unless students are expected to conduct research to complete the task.
6. Verify that the task or assessment item is clear, concise, and focused on the learning target.
7. Define the criteria that will be used to evaluate students' responses. If the question is open-ended, a scoring guide is needed.

Scenarios and Real-World Applications Tasks and Assessment Examples

This section provides examples of instructional tasks and assessment examples of scenarios, real-world situations, and authentic tasks for math, science, social studies, and language arts. These examples will hopefully spur your creativity to design your own instructional tasks or assessments using these types of interpretive materials.

In the multiple-choice questions below, the correct answers are in **bold type**.

Math Examples

Scenario

Example 1:

Kim solved the equation $\frac{2}{4}x = 16$ and got the answer 32. She knew that she was right, but when she checked her answer it did not work and she did not know why! Determine which explanation does NOT represent the correct justification for solving the equation.

a. Jeffrey thinks equations are balanced sometimes. Jeffrey states, "In solving $\frac{2}{4}x = 16$, you can either divide each side by $\frac{2}{4}$ or multiply each side by $\frac{2}{4}$ because division and multiplication are inverse operations."

b. Keisha writes, "In $\frac{2}{4}x = 16$, $\frac{2}{4}$ can also be 0.5. You will be doing the same operation if the equation has a fraction rather than a decimal."

c. Gregg states that there are two ways to solve $\frac{2}{4}x = 16$ because of the fraction. Instead of doing the inverse and dividing by $\frac{2}{4}$, multiply both sides by 4, then divide by 2, and you will get the same answer.

Example 2:

Monica, Tony, and Drew are all working to solve an order of operation problem on the board. The question states $-4 + 2^4 - (12 \div 3) + 3 \times 4$. Determine which student(s) found the correct answer.

Monica's work
$-4 + 2 = -2$
$(-2)^4 = 16$
$16 - (12 \div 3) = 12$
$12 + 3 = 15$
$15 \times 4 = 45$

So 45 must be the correct answer, because I worked from left to right, but made sure to do what is in the parentheses before the rest.

Tony's work
$12 \div 3 = 4$
$2^4 = 16$
$3 \times 4 = 12$
$-4 + 16 = 12$
$12 - 12 = 0$
$0 + 12 = 12$

So 12 must be the correct answer, because when you follow the order of operations you solve the contents of the parentheses; next you solve exponents; next you solve multiplication and division from left to right. Finally, you solve addition and subtraction from left to right.

Drew's work
$12 \div 3 = 4$
$2^4 = 16$
$3 \times 4 = 12$
$-4 + 16 = 12$
$4 + 12 = 16$
$12 - 16 = -4$

Negative 4 is the correct answer because of "Please Excuse My Dear Aunt Sally." First you do what is in parentheses. Then you solve exponents. Next you multiply, then divide, then add. Finally, you subtract. All of my friends know this saying, so it must be correct!

A. Which student(s) found the correct answer?

_____

B. For the student(s) who were incorrect, identify their mistake.

_____

_____

_____

Example 3:

Brandon goes to Buffalo Wild Wings and consumes a large number of wings. After three hours and five refills of his drink, he ate 12 barbecue wings, 18 teriyaki wings, 24 mango habanera wings, and 60 spicy wings. What is the rate of wing consumption per hour for Brandon's eating event?

a. 12 wings per hour

b. 36 wings per hour

c. 38 wings per hour

d. 60 wings per hour

Example 4:

Handsome Andy wants to buy his beautiful girlfriend, Susie, of three years, a Christmas gift. Susie expects a more expensive gift than last year. Andy sees two pairs of shoes that he knows she will like. One pair costs $50 with a 10% discount. The other pair costs $100 with a 55% discount.

A. Which pair of shoes is less expensive? Show your work.

_____

_____

B. Right before Andy makes the purchase, the salesperson says "Today only, for every $25 you spend before discounts, you receive $5.00 in store credit." Should Andy change his mind as to which shoes to purchase? Why or why not?

_____

_____

_____

Real-World Situation

Example 1:

I had friends come visit this weekend. Jamie brought a 12-pack case of her favorite Sunkist drink. June brought three bags of chips. I didn't like the Sunkist drinks so at the end of the night Jamie took three-quarters of the canned beverages home. How many canned drinks did she take home?

a. 3   c. 1½

b. 2   **d. 9**

Example 2:

Our principal took six students out for pizza, and they ordered two large pizzas. Each pizza was cut into 12 slices. Each person ate one piece from each pizza. After they finished their slices, our principal, a former math teacher, asked them how much pizza was eaten.

◆ Jill said 12/24 of the pizza was eaten.

◆ Adam said 14/12 of the pizza was eaten.

◆ Andy said 14 pieces.

Decide which person you agree with the most and explain your reasoning.

_____

_____

_____

_____

Example 3:

Our basketball team has won 12 of our first 20 games.

A. Investigate the ratio of wins to losses for the first 20 games.

B. Determine how many of its next 10 games the team must win in order to maintain the ratio of wins to losses.

_____

_____

Authentic Task

Example 1:

You want to get the best buy on a cell phone plan.

A. If you currently have a phone, compare the services and charges of your phone company to one other company. If not, select two cell phone companies to compare.

B. Using Excel or another software program, create a chart showing the factors that contribute to the total cost of the phone service.

C. Explain which phone is the best deal.

_____

_____

_____

Example 2:

Our school needs to construct a wheelchair ramp for the entrance to our gym. The school has decided to select the best design created by our class.

Your challenge:

◆ To research, test, and produce a ramp (either real size or small scale) to show the administrators at school.

Requirements:

◆ Write a three-page paper briefly describing two potential designs for the ramp. Identify the mathematical calculations used for the designs.

◆ Design and implement an experiment to test the effectiveness of each ramp.

◆ Determine the best design of the two which is supported by the results of your experiment.

◆ Develop a presentation for the administrators justifying why the design you chose would be the best solution.

Example 3

Our community celebrates our history by designing quilts.

A. Design a quilt using tessellations of three geometric figures. Use one of the online tessellation creators to develop your design.

B. Explain how your design represents our community values.

_____

_____

_____

_____

Science Examples

Scenario

Example 1:

A student in your science class states that the water we drink today is the same water dinosaurs drank millions of years ago.

A. Explain if this belief is true or false.

_____

_____

B. Use your knowledge about the water cycle to support your answer.

_____

_____

This example was presented by Martha Day, Rebecca Stobaugh, and Janet Tassell at a conference in 2010.

Example 2:

Which of the following examples is best explained by Newton's First Law?

a. A rocket is taking off from Earth, which pushes gases in one direction and the rocket in the other.

b. A rocket is sitting on the ground, preparing for take-off, and needs an outside force to overcome its inertia of a nonmoving object.

c. A rocket is accelerating through space and exerts a great amount of force because its mass and acceleration are so large.

Example 3:

Mr. and Mrs. Smith want to have a child. Based on their family history, they have some concerns. Mr. Smith's family has a history of carrying Huntington's disease. Huntington's disease is located on chromosome 4 and affects a person's ability to think, talk, and move. This disease is a dominant trait if carried.

A. If Mr. Smith is a carrier and Mrs. Smith is not, what is the probability of the couple having a child who will have Huntington's disease?

_____

B. What is the probability that Mr. and Mrs. Smith are both carriers? Please show and explain your work.

_____

_____

Real-World Situation

Example 1:

Yesterday, in our class, when lab partners discussed combining the elements Mg and Cl, there were different opinions on how to do it. Below is a summary of the discussions.

◆ Ben and Ed: "The goal is to get a valance number of 8. If Mg is 2 and Cl is 7, the two won't combine. They would get a total number of 9, which is too many."

◆ Charlie and Steve: "These two elements will combine if you use two Cl atoms and one Mg atom. The Mg would give one electron to each Cl."

◆ Ben and Ed: "You can't use two of one element and only one of the other. That would require two bonds."

◆ Charlie and Steve: "It must work because all of the elements would be balanced at 8 or 0."

Which pair of partners is correct and why?

_____

_____

_____

_____

_____

Example 2:

I was working in the yard this weekend and left a glass of water outside for an entire day. When I brought the glass of water inside, the amount of water in the glass had decreased. What is the cause of the decrease in water?

a. **evaporation**

b. condensation

c. precipitation

d. accumulation

Source: Day, Stobaugh, &Tassell, 2010

Authentic Task

Example 1:

New Age Construction Company builds reasonably priced new homes. To help make homes affordable, the company is looking to cut costs on wiring. It currently uses copper wire, which is a great conductor of electricity, but very expensive. New Age Construction Company is asking you to determine a new material that can be used for wiring. You must complete the following:

A. Select three new materials that could be a good alternative for the wiring.

_____

_____

_____

B. Describe how you would test each material.

_____

_____

_____

_____

C. Provide pricing for each material based on current market values.

_____

_____

_____

_____

Example 2:

Fifty dollars has been donated to our school to launch an environmental initiative to reduce, reuse, and/or recycle.

A. In your group, determine the best way to reduce, reuse, and/or recycle using no more than $50.

B. Using Prezi or another technology, create a persuasive presentation to show our school administrators and community leaders that your idea will have the largest impact.

Social Studies Examples

Scenario

Example 1:

In the late 1990s, a large influx of Bosnians relocated to a community. Due to this immigration, the community has Bosnian restaurants and groceries. This best demonstrates which theme of geography?

a. Location

b. Place

c. Human-environmental interaction

d. Movement

Example 2:

K-Mart has recently added retail stores in different communities in hopes of boosting profits. Wal-Mart noticed K-Mart's recent expansion and also began to add stores in other cities. This example is similar to which of the following historical events?

a. The Puritans' movement for religious freedom

b. The rivalry between Spain and England to gain wealth

c. The use of slaves to fuel the growing tobacco industry

d. The conflicts that occurred between the Indian tribes

Real-World Situation

Example 1:

America has a democratic government.

A. Select one group that you are a part of that has democratic qualities.

B. Describe three ways the group displays democratic principles.

_____

_____

C. Explain one aspect of the group that is undemocratic.

_____

_____

_____

_____

Example 2:

Our local hardware store has been losing business in the last few years.

A. Propose three possible reasons for this trend.

_____

_____

_____

B. Based on your understanding of economics, what is the best way to reverse this trend?

_____

_____

_____

_____

Authentic Task

Example 1:

It's election time in our community! Your task is to create a product that convinces teens to vote for a candidate.

A. Research the candidates running for office.

B. Select one candidate and create a product that creatively persuades teens to vote for your candidate.

Example 2:

Our school is going to host an Entrepreneurial Fair. During this event you will sell an item. Your goal is to generate more profit than the other participants.

- ◆ Generate a list of ideas of products that you think your classmates might buy.

- ◆ Select your product.

- ◆ Determine the cost of the product.

- ◆ Design your booth with appropriate advertisements.

- ◆ Sell your product!

After the fair, you will write a reflective essay identifying what strengths you have as an entrepreneur and what you would change if you were participating in the fair again.

Example 3:

An archeological dig has unearthed artifacts of an earlier civilization.

A. Examine the archeological dig site map and pictures of the artifacts.

B. Based on your examination, prepare a report detailing your conclusions on the following:

♦ Time period of the civilization

♦ Description of their culture, highlighting their values and beliefs

Language Arts Examples

Scenario

Example 1:

Juan's grandmother receives a water bill each month for about $30. This month, the water bill showed her owing $1,182.00. She called the plumber to check her pipes, and he found no abnormalities. She called the water company, which still requires her to pay the total amount of the bill. His grandmother asks Juan to write a letter to the water company on her behalf. What should Juan's letter include?

a. Clear details about the issue, facts supporting the findings, and a formal statement of the outcomes desired

b. Statement about his grandmother's character and details about the issue

c. A statement detailing the issue, a threat to beat up the water company's employees, and a formal statement of the outcomes desired

d. A quick summary of the issue, a refusal to pay the bill, and a picture of the water meter

Example 2:

Ms. Johnson's class wants to write a persuasive letter about the movie theater situation in Bluegrass, Kentucky. Their main point is:

"There is a need for another theater with competitive prices to be built in Bluegrass."

The class brainstormed a list of supporting ideas. Help the class select the best three supporting ideas from the list:

I. There is only one theater in Bluegrass, Movie Mania, which has a monopoly and thus has high ticket prices.

II. Underage students are often allowed to see R-rated movies at Movie Mania, which the parents in the community should be concerned about.

III. Movie Mania's parking lot isn't big enough; a new theater could have a bigger one.

IV. Movie Mania has a reputation for bad customer service, but doesn't care because the manager knows that customers don't have another choice of theaters nearby.

V. Many other theaters have more options for concessions, like pizza stands or ice cream vendors.

VI. Bluegrass has too many people to have just one theater, so the movies are always crowded.

Which of the above supporting ideas are critical to include in class's persuasive letter?

a. I, II, IV

b. II, III, VI

c. I, IV, VI

d. II, IV, V

Example 3:

Two locals are running for the office of mayor. Candidate A's platform is based on decreasing the unemployment rate. In a recent interview, she told a heart-wrenching story of how her own family nearly lost everything when the economy fell. She went into detail about her family's losses, hardship, and grief, stating, "I want to do whatever I can to make sure other families don't have to go through what we had to only a few short years ago."

Candidate A is most heavily relying on which rhetorical strategy?

a. ethos

b. logos

c. pathos

d. post hoc

Real-World Situation

Example 1:

Our school administration has decided to ban pep rallies during school hours. Write a paper with three persuasive arguments to explain why you agree or disagree with the school policy. Use supporting details and at least four quotes from students and/or faculty members to support your case.

Example 2:

The Great Gatsby addresses the theme of the "American dream."

A. Explain if the "American dream" has changed since the book was written.

_____

_____

_____

_____

B. Describe how you or someone in your family has tried to achieve the "American dream."

_____

_____

_____

_____

Authentic Task

Example 1:

Our state is considering legalizing gambling and allowing casinos.

A. Research the issue.

B. Decide if you approve or disapprove of this legislation.

C. Write a letter of support or disapproval. Decide the audience for your writing (e.g., the governor, the public, a legislator). Based on your audience, identify what letter format would be most effective.

Example 2:

Several students have been complaining about bullying in our school.

A. Identify reasons why these students might believe bullying is a problem in our school.

B. Create a satiric cartoon OR article to be published in the school newspaper to showcase the problem of bullying. If you choose a cartoon, you may use Toon Doon, Pixton, or another online comic generator.

Discuss

◆ Where have you previously observed scenarios, real-world examples, and authentic tasks being used as instructional tools or assessments?

◆ How are teachers in your building using scenarios, real-world examples, and authentic tasks?

◆ In your classroom, how could you use scenarios, real-world examples, and authentic tasks?

Take Action

◆ Design a scenario, real-world example, and authentic task that you could use as an instructional tool or assessment.

◆ Examine the instructional tasks and assessments you currently use. Where could you replace or implement an instructional activity or assessment with a scenario, real-world example, and/or authentic task to improve the quality of instruction in your classroom?

Visual Materials

The human mind, once stretched to a new idea, never goes back to its original dimensions.

—Oliver Wendell Holmes

Visuals are another source of materials for creating interpretive exercises. Images abound in our culture, from television shows to billboards. In schools, visuals from media, books, and a variety of other sources are used in instruction to build student understandings.

There are several benefits to using visuals. One benefit is that visuals assist beginning readers, English language learners, and students with reading disabilities by helping them understand the task through pictures instead of text. Many students who have difficulty with reading can express their knowledge through pictures and learn especially well from visuals. In addition, many students prefer to learn in a visual way. I personally first examine the diagrams in a technical guide and then, if necessary, read the instructions. Research has found that people process visuals 60,000 faster than text (3M Corporation, 2001). Thus, visuals assist in speedier student comprehension.

This chapter will describe different types of visual materials and how to use them to create high-level thinking opportunities. Recommendations for designing tasks and assessments using visual materials are provided, followed by multiple examples from several content areas.

Types of Visuals

There are several types of visuals that can be used in instructional tasks and assessments: illustrations, charts, data tables, maps, and diagrams. In some instances, visual materials can be combined with scenarios to create a challenging task. For example, students could be given a scenario of a scientific experiment with a data chart of unexpected results. Students could draw conclusions on what potentially caused those results. This section will focus on the many ways illustrations, charts, data tables, maps, and diagrams can be used in instructional tasks and assessments.

Illustrations or Objects

Illustrations, including advertisements, paintings, pictures, and cartoons, often provide vivid and captivating images for students to explore. Traditionally illustrations have been used in content areas like art class when examining paintings or perhaps in English classes when examining advertisements for persuasive techniques. However, illustrations can be used in all content areas.

Advertisements are a rich source for images. Students can analyze advertisements to identify persuasion techniques and examine whether the claims are accurate. Students can investigate using their knowledge of math and science to confirm the claims. For example, does a new exercise product produce results? Students can also examine advertisements from a historical perspective to identify common assumptions held at an earlier time period or draw conclusions about the culture of that time.

There are also many paintings and pictures that can be used as visual materials. A painting could be examined for clues in identifying the historical time period for an English or social studies class. Students can examine the similarities and differences between the paintings and the writing styles of a certain time period. A painting could be used as a stimulus for students to generate a creative story about what is happening in the painting or picture. In math class, students can examine mathematical principles in art. For example, when are geometric figures aesthetically pleasing in art? How do artists use mathematic ideas of proportion in paintings? In science, students can examine how paintings and pictures reflect scientific ideas of the historical time period. A new rising source of visuals is infographics, which are visual representations of information, data, or knowledge. Students can examine infographics created or design their own. A website called *Visual.ly* provides many infographics examples.

Cartoons are a way to inject humor and critical thinking into a class while providing another source of images. Students can examine cartoons to identify the cartoonist's point of view. Students can detect stereotypes, caricatures, and symbolism. Examining a cartoon with characters talking about how they answered a math problem, students could identify their mistake in reasoning. Teachers and students can draw their own cartoons or create them online using websites such as *ToonDoo* or *Make Beliefs Comix*. When students create their own cartoons, they can summarize information and profile their point of view on a topic.

In addition, a real object can be used as a visual. For example, students might analyze a fossil, old map, photograph, piece of art, or postcard to draw conclusions about how it was created, how old it is, and where it comes from. Students could become detectives trying to unearth clues about a mysterious object.

Charts and Data Tables

Another source of images is data tables and charts. Data tables organize numbers or information in a systematized fashion. With information organized, charts can then be created if desired. Charts are graphical representations of data. There are numerous types of charts: line charts, pie charts, organizational charts, and flow charts. While charts are often used in math and science classes, many content areas can use charts and tables to organize information about population trends, public opinion, temperature, interest rates, stock market prices, scientific experiment results, and mathematical data.

Charts and data tables challenge students to cognitively process the information at high levels as they interpret data and draw conclusions. Charts and tables are often used to persuade audiences. Students must learn to scrutinize these, as data are not always represented accurately. Inaccurate representations of data can lead to faulty conclusions. Students can also be given a data table or chart with headings not completely identified. Students could generate possible headings for the data table or chart.

Students can also collect and create their own data tables and charts to depict information in an illustrative form. In social studies, students could survey others to determine the key political issues affecting teens or which environmental solution would best address a local problem. In English class, students could create a data table or chart to support their persuasive argument.

Maps and Diagrams

Finally, maps and diagrams provide numerous images for students to evaluate. Maps are a representation of the earth's surface often showing direction, size, or distance. There are climate, economic, resource, physical, political, road, and topographical maps. In English, students can examine the geographical location of the setting of a novel and assess if and how the geography affected the plot development. In science and social studies classes, students can examine maps to determine how geography impacts settlement patterns.

A diagram is used to show a symbolic representation of information. Often diagrams are used to better visualize information. Many diagrams have been created to represent information on various topics, including the human body, plot development, and the technical structure of objects like a spacecraft. In addition, many graphic organizers are used, including cause-and-effect organizers, fishbone diagrams, Venn comparison diagrams, and concept maps. Students can create their own diagrams to build their conceptual understanding. They can also analyze various diagrams on the same topic, identifying similarities and differences between the representations while finding irregularities. Teachers can give students several diagrams to analyze and have the students select which diagram best represents the information.

Higher-Level Thinking

As with all interpretive exercises, since the introductory information provides new material for students to understand, minimally all tasks and assessments would be on the Understand level of Bloom's taxonomy. At the Understand level, students can interpret the meaning and draw conclusions from the visual materials. They can compare and contrast various visuals. When examining visuals, students can identify examples or non-examples of an identified concept. For instance, students could circle all the pictures that represent early Greek architecture or tessellations. Students could create an example that would represent a given data set or chart. Also, students could classify visual materials in various categories and provide defensible reasons to justify their classifying system—for example, when investigating fossils, students could decide to group all the fossils that showed marine life in one category. Students can use visuals to make analogies or metaphors of concepts studied. For instance, how is a picture of a sculpture like a character in a novel? Based on information from a data table or chart, students can also make predictions about what could happen in the future or how the data could impact other factors. For example, based on a chart of a country's deforestation trends, students could hypothesize how the economy and living conditions are currently being affected and will be impacted in the future if the trends continue.

Tasks on the Apply level of Bloom's taxonomy usually require students to use a skill. For example, students can use visual materials to create calculations, identify correct sentence diagrams, and determine longitude and latitude on maps. In addition, students could devise formulas to represent data sets.

Students can also engage in analysis and evaluation. When examining paintings, pictures, and cartoons, students can be challenged to identify possible biases or points of view. Students can also identify errors in visual materials. After reading, students could design their own graphic representation or diagram of the written material. To evaluate, students can select an image that best represents a historical time period and defend their choice. Students could select and explain which exercise plan depicted in a chart best meets the particular needs of a nursing home patient.

At the Create level of Bloom's taxonomy, students can design visual materials to bolster their persuasive remarks, to support their scientific recommendations, or to express their viewpoint. This might involve students taking a survey and collecting data or designing their own political cartoon.

Design Tips

Some tips are provided below to assist you in designing interpretive materials using images.

- Find images on the Internet. There is a wealth of visuals available in textbooks and on the Internet. Due to the ease of searching the Internet, it is a quick way to access images. Most search engines provide an option to restrict the search to images only, producing numerous images for the teacher or student to select from for an instructional task or assessment. However, be aware of copyright protections on images.

- Use new images. As previously mentioned, to ensure higher-level thinking, use images that students have not already analyzed. If you use a familiar image, ensure that students are thinking about it in a new way.

- Make sure that the image is required to answer the assessment. Since the image will be in the introductory material, the assessment or task should require students to use the image in some way. If the students can answer the question without looking at the graphic, then the image is unnecessary.

- Use a clear image. Whether the image is found online or copied from a book, make sure the graphic is clear, particularly if it will be reproduced. When images are copied or scaled to differing sizes or when color graphics are printed in black and white, they may become distorted, impacting the clarity of the visuals. Visuals need to be large enough for students to appropriately interpret them. Some teachers include small, black-and-white visuals on an assessment, but also use a larger color version on the computer screen.

For steps to design assessments with visual materials see Figure 5.1.

Figure 5.1 **Steps to Design Visual Materials Assessments**

1. Identify a learning target or standard.
2. Search online or in texts for visual materials that align to the learning target or standard.
3. Select printed materials that are new to the students.
4. Make sure visuals are clear.
5. Verify that the question requires students to understand the visual before answering the question.
6. Check to make sure that the assessment item is appropriate for students' knowledge and skill level.
7. Ensure that the assessment item is clear, concise, and focused on the learning target.
8. If it is an open-ended task or assessment, define the criteria that will be used to evaluate students' responses.

Visual Tasks
and
Assessment Examples

This section provides examples of instructional tasks and assessments using illustrations, objects, maps, diagrams, charts, and data tables for the math, science, social studies, and language arts content areas. Through examining these examples, you can get ideas to design your own instructional tasks or assessments using these types of interpretive materials.

In the multiple-choice questions below, the correct answers are in **bold type**.

Math Examples

Illustrations

<u>Example 1:</u>

Which of the following figures have rotational symmetry?

Object A:

Object B:

Object C:

Object D:

a. Object A

b. Object B

c. Object C

d. Object D

Example 2:

 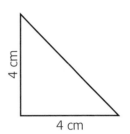

Examine the triangles above.

A. Find the area of the three triangles.

_____

B. Make inferences about the relationships among the side lengths and the areas of the triangles.

_____
_____
_____
_____
_____
_____

Example 3:

Jan wants to put a new window in the front of her house. The window she has picked is shown to the right. The window company needs to know the area and perimeter of the window in order to give her a price estimate. Calculate the total area and the perimeter of the window. Which equation below represents the correct answer?

a. $8 + .5\pi$

b. $8 + 4\pi$

c. $8 + 2\pi$

d. $12 + .5\pi$

Example 4:

How is the image to the right a metaphor for the order of operations? Describe three similarities.

_____

_____

_____

_____

_____

_____

_____

_____

_____

_____

Charts and Data Tables

Example 1:

Adam is going to purchase a new car but is concerned about the car's gas mileage due to high fuel prices. He finds three cars that are possible choices within his budget. The following table tells the the average miles per gallon (mpg) of gasoline each car gets. If he plans on driving 70 miles per week, which car would be the best choice? Explain your reasoning.

Car	mpg
Mini Cooper	32
Ford F-150 Pickup	19
Toyota Camry Hybrid	41

_____

_____

_____

_____

_____

_____

_____

Example 2:

A. For the three points given, what type of equation would satisfy these points? (linear, quadratic, exponential, etc.)

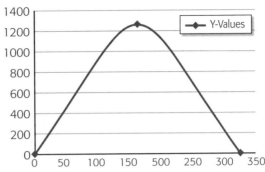

_____

_____

B. Describe the motion of a real-world example that would follow the equation graphed above, assuming that the x-axis represents time and the y-axis represents distance.

_____

_____

_____

_____

_____

_____

Maps and Diagrams

Example 1:

Which scenario would best describe the graphic?

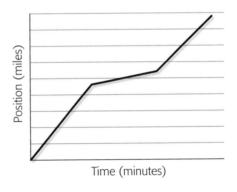

a. **The driver is traveling on an interstate. She slows down in a construction zone. At the end of the zone, she returns to the original speed.**

b. The driver slows to a stop at a red light. He waits three minutes for the light to change. He then accelerates out of the intersection.

c. The driver accelerates onto a highway. She speeds up to pass a slow-moving truck. She then slows down to a moderate speed.

d. The driver travels at a moderate speed. He accelerates to make it through an intersection before the light changes. He then returns to the original speed.

Science Examples

Illustrations

Example 1:

Billy bought a new television and needs to move it into his house, which is pictured to the right. Which simple machine is the best choice to help Billy move his television inside?

a. wedge

b. wheel and axle

c. level

d. inclined plane

Source: Day, Stobaugh, & Tassell, 2010

Example 2:

The following pictures are examples of simple machines:

A. Describe two similarities between the machines.

_____

_____

_____

_____

_____

_____

_____

B. Explain one difference between the machines.

_____

_____

_____

_____

_____

_____

Charts and Data Tables

Example 1:

Year	Percentage of Pollution in the Air
2020	0.91%
2023	1.2%
2026	5.9%
2029	6.0%
2032	6.2%

The table above represents the percentage of air pollution in Utopia, a country located in a remote rural area. What could be three possible reasons that would explain this data?

_____

_____

_____

_____

_____

_____

_____

_____

Maps and Diagrams

Example 1:

The image to the right best depicts what?

  a. food chain

  b. adaptation

  c. migration

  d. prey

Example 2:

Position (miles) / Time (minutes)

Which scenario would best describe the graphic above?

a. Ian walked three miles before stopping to take a five-minute break. He then ran two more miles.

b. Ian ran three miles before getting tired. He walked two more miles.

c. Ian walked three miles as a warm-up. He then ran two more miles.

d. Ian ran three miles before stopping to take a five-minute break. He then walked two more miles.

Example 3

We have studied the human skeletal system already. Examine this diagram of a moose.

A. Identify three similarities between the skeletal system of a moose and a human. For each, explain why these similarities exist.

_____

_____

_____

_____

_____

_____

_____

B. Identify one difference between the skeletal systems of a moose and a human. Propose a logical reason for why the difference exists.

_____

_____

_____

_____

Social Studies Examples

Illustrations

Example 1:

The cartoon best represents which of the following during the settlement period?

a. The establishment of Jamestown, which led to the first Thanksgiving

b. The conflict over land between the Native Americans and the settlers

c. The pursuit of happiness and prosperity during the 1600s by the Pilgrims and Puritans

Example 2:

If this image came from a wall of a tomb, in which kingdom was this tomb most likely built?

a. Old Kingdom

b. Middle Kingdom

c. Gold Kingdom

d. New Kingdom

Charts and Data Tables

Example 1:

Using the graph, which concept is most likely represented?

a. law of supply

b. law of demand

c. market clearing price

d. opportunity cost

Example 2:

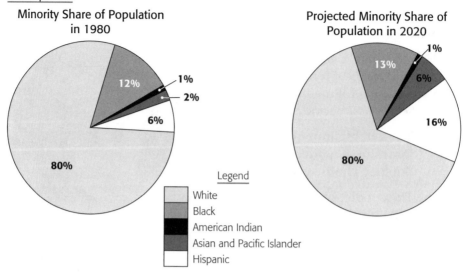

Minority Share of Population in 1980

12%   1%
           2%
      6%
80%

Projected Minority Share of Population in 2020

13%   1%
       6%
80%   16%

Legend
White
Black
American Indian
Asian and Pacific Islander
Hispanic

Source: United States Census Bureau

Based on the two charts above, which ethnicity would you predict to have the largest share of the minority population in 2030?

a. Black

b. Hispanic

c. Asian

d. American Indian

Maps and Diagrams

Example 1:

Marsha is planning a trip to India. She can use this map for which of the following purposes

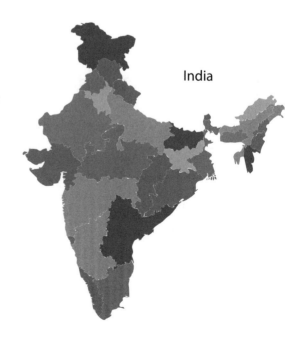

India

a. determining the major cities in the regions

b. finding the boundary lines between countries

c. identifying coastal cities

d. finding points of high elevation

Example 2

Map projections, like the one above, show a representation of Earth on a flat surface.

A. Explain three reasons why the cartographer might have created this map projection.

_____

_____

_____

_____

_____

_____

_____

B. How might biases or perspective have impacted this creation?

_____

_____

_____

_____

_____

_____

Example 3:

South Africa is a growing country.

A. Determine the best place to locate a new hotel for visitors who want to see the natural landscape of South Africa.

_____

_____

_____

B. Use two maps to support your decision.

Language Arts Examples

Illustrations

Example 1:

Using the painting as a reference, which American literary period is best represented?

a. naturalism

b. transcendentalism

c. realism

d. romanticism

Example 2

People or characters in a book often remind us of other things.

A. Choose one of the two images shown above that you feel best represents the emotions of the female character in the text we have been reading.

_____

B. Determine three reasons why the image is the best depiction of her emotions and support your reasons with textual evidence.

_____

_____

_____

C. Briefly describe another image that comes to mind that you believe could represent her emotions.

_____

_____

Example 3:

In Mary Shelley's frame-story novel *Frankenstein*, the original setting is the Swiss Alps (Figure 1).

A. In a brief paragraph, describe how the original setting relates to at least two themes in the text.

B. Examine the two pictures below. If the setting of the novel were modern-day New York (Figure 2), what kind of turn might the plot take? Provide at least two pieces of evidence from the text that would support your claim.

C. Explain how changing the setting of the story from Figure 1 to Figure 2 might affect the character development of the creature. Provide at least two pieces of evidence from the text that would support your claim.

Figure 1

Figure 2

Charts and Data Tables

Example 1:

Character	Role	Synopsis
Pap	Huck's father	Pap is an illiterate drunk who represents a poor family structure. He denounces Huck's education and beats him.
Huck Finn	Protagonist	Huck is an independent young boy who struggles with society's expectations and his own morals. Despite society's belief system, Huck learns to accept Jim (the slave) as any other man.
Jim	Huck's companion, a house slave	Jim is a runaway slave who is traveling with Huck. From the very beginning, Jim is caring and compassionate. He may be seen as the most respectable character in the novel.
Tom	Huck's best friend	Tom is Huck's best friend, who doesn't appear until near the end of the novel. Tom's social status is upper-class, he has a heightened imagination, and his adventures are often self-centered and cruel.

Before we begin reading *Adventures of Huckleberry Finn*, use the chart above to determine which character(s) are round characters.

a. Huck

b. Jim

c. Pap and Huck

d. Tom and Huck

Example 2:

Comic	Love It	OK	Hate It
Family Circus	130	40	2
Blondie	129	40	3
Dennis the Menace	119	50	3
Classic Peanuts	109	54	9
For Better or for Worse	65	80	27
Dilbert	20	92	60

Our local newspaper surveyed its readers on their opinions of the cartoons that the paper prints. The chart above shows the results of the survey.

A. Examine several examples of each of the cartoons.

B. Based on your understanding of the community and the cartoons, propose two reasons for these results.

_____

_____

_____

_____

_____

_____

Example 3:

Poem Descriptions			
Poem 1	Poem 2	Poem 3	Poem 4
◆ relatively short ◆ written to be sung ◆ contains four-line stanzas ◆ often written about love, death, or the supernatural	◆ lyric poem containing fourteen lines ◆ three coordinate quatrains ◆ concluding couplet	◆ Japanese-style poem ◆ contains three un-rhymed lines of 5, 7, and 5 syllables ◆ often creates images of nature ◆ originated in the 16th century	◆ very long poem ◆ tells a story of a heroic figure ◆ setting of the poem is often large-scale (world-wide) ◆ action usually involves superhuman deeds

Given the characteristics of each of the poems in this chart, which poem is a ballad poem?

a. **Poem 1**   c. Poem 3

b. Poem 2   d. Poem 4

Maps and Diagrams

Example 1:

Examine the Business Plan diagram. What are three similarities between the processes of writing a research paper and creating a business plan?

_____

_____

_____

_____

_____

_____

_____

_____

_____

_____

_____

_____

Example 2:

I. He | is
            \ kind

II. She | drives
              \ often

III. boys | are \ funny
          \ The

Which of the above sentences is diagrammed incorrectly?

a. I

b. II

c. III

Discuss

   ◆ Where have you previously observed visual materials embedded into instructional tasks or assessments?

   ◆ How are teachers in your building using visual materials?

   ◆ In your classroom, how could you use visual materials?

Take Action

   ◆ Design an instructional task or assessment using an illustration, object, data table, chart, map, or diagram.

   ◆ Examine the instructional tasks and assessments you currently use. Where could you replace an instructional task or assessment with one that includes visual materials to improve the quality of your instruction?

Quotations

In thinking critically, we take command of the meanings we create.
—Richard Paul and Linda Elder

A third way to increase the level of cognitive complexity in instructional tasks and assessments is by using quotations. Teachers can use short quotes, a few sentences long, or longer passages from written sources. Additionally, media can provide quotes through news and television shows, movies, and songs. Short quotes, passages, and media clips are other ways to provide introductory materials in an interpretive exercise in order to infuse critical thinking into classroom tasks and assessments.

Many of the questions on standardized tests and materials in college courses include quotes, interpretive readings, and media clips, with students expected to make thoughtful inferences and determine perspectives. This expectation goes beyond the traditional worksheets and textbook end-of-the-section questions that require students to find the correct answers without deeply processing the reading. Through understanding and analyzing quotes, students build stronger conceptual understandings and thinking skills.

This chapter will profile different types of quotes and show how they can be embedded into instructional experiences to create high-level thinking opportunities. Recommendations for designing tasks and assessments using quotes are provided, followed by multiple examples from several content areas.

Types of Quotations

Short Quotes

Short quotes are a few sentences in length. A quote from a student or a famous person can provide an immediate way to initiate a lesson, become a classroom activity, or be used as an assessment. Quotes can be used in all subject areas. For instance, William Shakespeare in *The Tempest* wrote, "Hell is empty and all the devils are here." This quote could easily relate to content in several subjects.

- ◆ **Social studies:** What time period in history could be characterized by this quote?

- ◆ **Language arts:** What characters in a text would probably agree with this quote?

- ◆ **Vocational studies:** Which modern-day company would exemplify this idea?

- ◆ **Science:** What actions in science could be described by this quote?

Passages

Longer reading passages can also be used including primary sources, literature passages, and informational sources (e.g., journals, web pages, newspapers, magazine articles). Under the Common Core State Standards, teachers of all subjects are expected to teach literacy. Thus, it is appropriate that all subject areas incorporate reading excerpts and passages into classroom instruction.

Primary sources provide firsthand testimony from someone who lived during a certain time period. Primary sources can be used in social studies classes to examine feelings and viewpoints during a particular era. Language arts teachers can use primary sources as a main text or to build prior knowledge before the class reads another text from the same time period. Science teachers can use primary sources to showcase scientific perspectives during certain eras in history. Students can also examine the writer's point of view and assumptions, while looking for inaccurate statements in the writing.

Teachers can integrate a variety of forms of literature, including novels, poems, dramas, and short stories. If the texts are lengthy, classes could examine an excerpt from the work. Most students love stories and poems that relate to students' interests. For instance, students can determine if a poem written by Eric Rose, or as he likes to be called "Mr. R.," on his "Math Story" website entitled "Hypotenuse" correctly describes the hypotenuse. Students could even write their own original poem on the topic.

There is also an abundance of informational sources in texts and online for teachers to use as supplementary materials for passages. For example, students could read passages from *Bloodletting Instruments in the National Museum of History and Technology* by Audrey Davis. In a social studies class, students could examine the impact of the practice of bloodletting on the culture and how this medical procedure emerged and waned. In science class, students can examine how this practice impacted patients' health.

To prepare for the academic writing expected in college, students can critique academic journal articles to help them become a better writer themselves. In addition, web pages, newspaper articles, and magazines showcase current perspectives and information that can connect to concepts being studied. Since selecting quality sources is an important skill, students can examine informational sources to assess their accuracy. There are several websites that are "fake" or "spoofs." For example, a site titled Dihydrogen Monoxide—DHMO Homepage claims that dihydrogen monoxide, otherwise known as water, is dangerous, which it is not. With the plethora of informational sources, students need to practice identifying quality sources of information.

Media Clips

A third source of engaging quotes is media clips. Online media, movie and television clips, songs, and your own footage provide many sources of media clips. Students often enjoy these instructional tasks and assessments because they are visually interesting and include sound and/or music and sometimes drama. For teachers, the Internet provides a multitude of free media clips. A recent Internet search for a video on balancing chemical equations produced 589,000 video options. In addition, many search engines will alert you if new videos are posted on an identified topic. The ease of acquiring media clips makes this resource one that can be effortlessly integrated into classroom instruction.

Using media clips from online is a great way of making real-world connections to your content. YouTube, CNN, local news stations, and a variety of companies produce online media daily that can be connected to what is being learned in the class. English classes can examine how current news applies to themes in literature. In science, students can examine news reports about new drugs and science inventions that apply to concepts studied. In math and science classes, students can examine how media use math and science to inform and persuade the public.

Movie and television clips are another interesting way to make connections between the lesson content and popular movies and television shows. For example, how are the governments in *The Hunger Games*, *Star Wars*, and America similar and different? In math, after watching a clip from the movie *Moneyball*, students could determine what statistics they would collect on athletes in a certain sport to predict their success.

Song lyrics often show the feelings of people. Using lyrics in class is a way to analyze perspectives and assumptions. It also appeals to students and their interest in music. In social studies and language arts classes, students can examine song lyrics to identify opinions during a historical period. In addition, students can make connections between current music lyrics and viewpoints of historical people, events, or novels. For example, students can make connections between a country music song and Thomas Jefferson's agrarian beliefs.

Many songs provide a way for students to learn basic concepts. "Why Does the Sun Shine?" is an example of a song and a video that teach the purpose of the sun. A recent search for songs about the quadratic equation revealed 407,000 songs available online. With a proliferation of songs available, students can analyze songs to determine if they are accurate. Students can also create their own songs to demonstrate their understandings. Students can take a current tune and create their own lyrics for the music. In my class, students took the tune of "The Itsy Bitsy Spider" and wrote lyrics about the "Itsy Bitsy" Pilgrims. Students can also use software such as Garage Band to creatively design their own music or podcasts about content.

With smart phone applications and other technologies that can record video, students can make their own videos. At a recent baseball practice, I was asked to video a pitcher warming up. The pitcher wanted to use the video of him along with a later added narration to explain how Newton's laws of motion were involved in the pitching and catching. While the assignment only required him to identify one law of motion, the student became so interested in the project that he planned to explain how all three of Newton's laws were shown in the pitching and catching video.

Higher-Level Thinking

Quotes, passages, and media clips can provide ways to reach higher-level thinking. Since the quotes, passages, or clips are new to the students, the task or assignment would be at least on the Understand level of Bloom's taxonomy. At this level, one way to assess comprehension of the introductory materials is by asking students to summarize information or make inferences. Another option is to require students to mentally make connections between the introductory materials and background information. Additionally, students could be asked to identify or provide another example of a concept in a quote. Using two quotes, passages, or media clips, students could compare and contrast the informational sources. Furthermore, after reading the quote, students can select who might have authored the quote.

On the Analyze level of Bloom's taxonomy, passages and quotes often have sections that are irrelevant to the assessment. Students can practice eliminating information in the quotes that is not relevant to the task or identifying misconceptions mentioned. Students can also organize information from a passage or media clip in a diagram. Through their reading and listening to media sources, students can be challenged to identify biases, assumptions, intentions, or points of view. At the Evaluate level, tasks can engage students in the decision-making process by identifying criteria and ranking options. For example, students could select which informational source best represents the achievements of a famous author or leader. In science, students can select which media clip best explains the rock cycle.

Design Tips

To assist you in developing interpretive materials using quotations, passages, and media, design tips are listed below.

◆ When selecting quotes and passages, consider the reading abilities of the students. Sometimes, reading passage or quotes from different time periods or from other countries can be difficult to read. If quotes or a reading passage are used as an assessment, the reading abilities of the students could affect their score.

◆ Availability of quotes. Searching online for the quotes about the content taught will yield a variety of options. Other ways to capture quotes is by interviewing your principal, other teachers, or students. Students can determine if the interviewee had any misconceptions or a different perspective about the content. An interview could also be captured on video to show the class.

◆ Connect to student interests. When possible, relate quotes to students' interests. Often famous celebrities make comments that can connect to the content of class lessons. For example, Lil Wayne, a rap star, stated, "I got ice in my veins, blood in my eyes, hate in my heart, love in my mind." This quote could be integrated to connect to themes or characters in literature and history. Connecting to students' interests and daily experiences reminds students of the current applications of the content.

For steps on designing these types of items, see Figure 6.1.

Figure 6.1 Steps to Design

1. Identify a learning target or standard.

2. Search for a quote, passage, or media excerpt that is new to the students and aligns to the standard or learning target.

3. Check to make sure the assessment item is appropriate for the examinees' development, knowledge, skill level, and academic experience.

4. Verify that an assessment item is clear, concise, and focused on the learning target or standard.

5. If the assessment requires an open-ended student response, define the criteria that will be used to evaluate students' responses.

Quotes, Passages, and Media Examples of Tasks and Assessment Examples

This section provides examples of instructional tasks and assessment examples using quotes, passages, and media in the math, science, social studies, and language arts content areas. When reviewing these examples, consider ways you can use these types of interpretive materials in your classroom.

In the multiple-choice questions below, the correct answers are in **bold type**.

Math Examples

Short Quote

Example 1:

Someone said, "⅝ of people are bad at fractions." Could this be true?

   a. Yes, because most people are bad at fractions.

   b. Yes, 5 is greater than 4; therefore more people are bad at fractions than good at fractions.

   c. **No, you cannot have 5 people if there are only 4 in a group.**

   d. No, more people are good at fractions than bad at fractions.

Example 2:

It has been said, "Why do we believe that in all matters the odd numbers are more powerful?" What could be meant by this statement?

Passage

Example 1:

After reading the story *The King's Big Foot*, explain your thoughts as to why standardized units are needed. Describe a situation in your life beyond school where standardized units were important for a task.

Example 2:

The article called "The World's Fastest Car" describes a car that travels at 1,000 miles per hour. Using information from the article, answer the following questions.

A. How many revolutions per hour will each wheel make? _____

B. How many revolutions per mile will each wheel make? _____

Article: "The World's Fastest Car," *Science World*, September 5, 2011, pp. 8–9

Media Clip Example

Example 1:

On the video clip, Jen is an extreme couponer who saved a large amount of money on a shopping trip.

A. Based on information in the video clip, calculate the amount she saved using proportions.

_____

B. If Jen pays 6 percent tax on her groceries before the discounts are taken, what would be the total amount of her bill? Please show all work.

_____

C. Challenge: Take a tip from Jen or research other money-saving tips and see how much money you can save on your next purchase. Share with the class your tip and how much money you saved.

_____

Video link: www.youtube.com/watch?v=ZT_8NzK5F7I

Example 2:

After watching the following video clips from movies and television where math is used incorrectly, choose one of the options below.

Choice #1
A. Select either *The Wizard of Oz, Star Trek*, or the newscast with the pie graph clip.
B. Explain the error(s) and then show the correct mathematical process.
Choice #2
A. Find another television show or movie that uses math incorrectly.
B. Explain the error(s) and then show the correct mathematical process.

Video link: www.youtube.com/watch?v=mlnLRKO3zII

Science Examples

Short Quote

Example 1:

"I get tan in the summer because the sun is closer to Earth and the rays are more intense."

   a. This statement is true. The sun is closer to Earth in the summer, making the rays more intense.

   b. This statement is true. The sun is brighter in the summer, making it feel hotter.

   c. This statement is false. The sun is farther away from Earth in the summer than in the winter.

   d. This statement is false. The angle of Earth allows the sun's rays to be more concentrated.

Example 2:

The Wright brothers stated, "So many people end up fixated on doing things right, that they end up doing nothing at all." How does their statement connect to the scientific method?

_____

_____

_____

_____

_____

_____

Example 3:

Charles Darwin stated, "It is not the strongest of the species that survives, nor the most intelligent that survives. It is the one that is the most adaptable to change." What term is best described in the above quote?

   a. evolution

   b. genetic variation

   c. extinction

   d. naturalism

Passage

<u>Example 1:</u>

Read the two lab reports: "Experemint 10" (sic) and "Identification of a Compound Using Melting and Boiling Points."

A. Identify at least six criteria you would use to evaluate the quality of a science lab report.

_____

_____

_____

B. Explain how each of the reports meets the criteria.

_____

_____

_____

_____

Lab report link: http://homepage.smc.edu/gallogly_ethan/sample_lab_reports.htm

<u>Example 2:</u>

The article "Color Change" discusses the reasons why the hot spring in Yellowstone has changed colors.

A. What is the reason for this change?

_____

_____

_____

_____

B. What is an example in your community that is experiencing a similar impact?

_____

_____

_____

Article: "Color Change," *Science World*, September 5, 2011, pp. 14–16

Media Clip

Example 1:

Complete either of the tasks below based on your observation from the video.

Choice #1
After watching the skating accidents, choose one accident from the video. A. Describe the physics behind the accident. B. Explain how the incident might be avoided by using your knowledge of physics.
Choice #2
Select an accident represented in a book, movie, song, or in your personal life. A. Describe the physics behind the accident. B. Explain how the incident might be avoided by using your knowledge of physics.

Video link: www.youtube.com/watch?v=Sqgvbmej6IM

Example 2:

In the television cooking episode there is an accident with a kitchen towel. Using your knowledge of chemistry, explain whether a chemical or physical change occurred.

_____

_____

_____

_____

Video link: www.youtube.com/watch?v=kMfR76GVBuk

Social Studies Examples

Short Quote

Example 1:

"I work on a farm. Sometimes members of our group use my land to harvest certain crops. Together we own the machinery to run our farms, which saves money." This quote could have been made by an owner of what type of farm?

a. mixed farm

b. collective farm

c. tenant farm

d. organic farm

Example 2:

Karl Marx stated, "The proletarians have nothing to lose but their chains.... Workers of the world, unite!" This statement refers to complaints made during what reformation?

 a. Industrial Reformation

 b. Protestant Reformation

 c. Counter-Reformation

 d. Commercial Reformation

Example 3:

The following statement was written by a student to summarize the French and Indian War: "In the 1740s, the French and the British became interested in the Ohio River Valley. To block British claims in the region, the French built forts from Lake Ontario to the Ohio River. The British responded by building a fort of their own in Canada. With the intention of expelling the French, a young Virginian, George Washington, led troops toward the Ohio River in the spring of 1754." Which is an incorrect piece of information?

 a. "In the 1740s..."

 b. "... a fort of their own in Canada."

 c. "... from Lake Ontario to the Ohio River."

 d. "... a young Virginian, George Washington, led troops ... "

Example 4:

"If a noble has knocked out the tooth of a noble of his own rank, they shall knock out his tooth. But if he has knocked out a commoner's tooth, he shall pay one-third mina of silver."—*Code of Hammurabi* What can be determined about the *Code of Hammurabi*?

 a. Punishments may be different for different social classes.

 b. All men equally received corporal punishment for their misdeeds.

 c. Fines were preferable to corporal punishment.

Passage

Example 1:

In the Native American fable titled *Another Lakota Creation Story*, which aspect of culture is the focus of the reading?

a. beliefs

b. crafts and arts

c. languages

d. traditions

Example 2:

Historians identify many people, events, and ideas that caused World War I. Decide which was the most significant cause of World War I.

A. Decide the criteria you will use to determine what is the most significant cause of the war.

_____

_____

_____

B. Use several informational sources to identify the top four potential causes.

_____

_____

_____

_____

C. Explain how each cause meets the criteria you identified.

_____

_____

_____

_____

D. Describe which cause, based on your research, is the most significant cause of World War I.

_____

_____

_____

_____

Media Clip

Example 1:

After listening to Martin Luther King's speech, create a diagram showing how King's ideas intersected with the early American colonists' desire for freedom.

Example 2:

After watching a political debate, decide which candidate won.

A. Develop criteria to determine how you will evaluate the candidates.

_____

_____

_____

_____

B. Rank the candidates on how they met your criteria.

_____

_____

_____

_____

C. Explain your rankings.

_____

_____

_____

_____

Language Arts Examples

Short Quotes

Example 1:

The following passage uses what type of figurative language?

"Our camera noticed the blood nourishing our eyes."

a. personification

b. simile

c. metaphor

d. allusion

Example 2:

Novelist Julien Green said, "Our life is a book that writes itself and whose principal themes sometimes escape us. We are like characters in a novel who do not always understand what the author wants of them."

A. Explain two ideas that support Green's quote.

_____

_____

_____

_____

B. Think of your life as a book. Determine a theme for yourself and explain two ways that that particular theme corresponds with your life.

_____

_____

_____

_____

Example 3:

"How wonderful it is that nobody need wait a single moment before starting to improve the world."

—Anne Frank

Based on this quote, which vocabulary term would best describe Anne Frank's outlook on life?

a. optimistic

b. radical

c. pessimistic

d. conservative

Example 4:

> *"I am a woman in process. I'm just trying like everybody else. I try to take every conflict, every experience, and learn from it. Life is never dull."*
> —Oprah Winfrey

From what character in the Wife of Bath's Tale would you most likely hear a statement like this?

a. The Queen

c. Wife of Bath

b. The Hag

d. Dancing Women

Passage

Example 1:

> *"For as much as government can do and must do, it is ultimately the faith and determination of the American people upon which this nation relies. It is the kindness to take in a stranger when the levees break, the selflessness of workers who would rather cut their hours than see a friend lose their job which sees us through our darkest hours."*
> —President Barack Obama's inauguration speech, 2008

What rhetorical appeal is used in this portion of the speech?

a. logos

c. pathos

b. ethos

d. bandwagon

Example 2:
Read the editorial.

A. Identify one claim in the editorial.

_____

_____

B. Briefly describe two pieces of reason or evidence the editorial uses to support the claim.

_____

_____

_____

C. Identify one claim that is unsupported with reasons or evidence.

_____

_____

Example 3:

Read "Manifesto: The Mad Farmer Liberation Front" by Wendell Berry.

A. Using at least three examples from the poem, explain what kind of lifestyle Wendell Berry is advocating.

_____

_____

_____

_____

_____

B. Using at least three examples from the poem, explain whether you would follow Wendell Berry's advice in this poem or not.

_____

_____

_____

_____

_____

Example 4:

Read Emily Dickinson's poem "A Bird came down the Walk." What does the bird symbolize in the poem?

a. **hope**   c. pride

b. fear   d. joy

Media Clip

Example 1:

In the video *Three Cheers for Catherine the Great*, what does Sara mean at the end of the video when she says, "Sometimes no presents are the best presents"?

a. **Sometimes presents can be doing something nice for someone.**

b. Sometimes "no presents" are better because presents are bad.

c. Sometimes people do not like to get presents.

d. Sometimes it is too much work to give presents.

Example 2:

In a spoof pitch of a reality TV show called *Child Island*, Jamie Kennedy sits down with a group of parents and offers their kids an opportunity to be a part of the show. When one parent speaks up about her concern for her child's safety, Jamie responds with this statement: "Hey, safe kids is a boring show!" After reading *The Hunger Games*, compare and contrast the desire for entertainment as shown in Kennedy's show with that of Panem.

A. Discuss at least two similarities between the role of entertainment in today's society and in Panem, using specific evidence to support your claims.

_____

_____

_____

_____

B. Discuss at least two differences between the role of entertainment in today's society and in Panem, using specific evidence to support your claims.

_____

_____

_____

_____

Web link: www.youtube.com/watch?v=3xTJ6GoBuCU

Discuss

◆ How are other teachers in your school using quotes, passages, and media in instructional tasks and assessments?

◆ In your classroom, how could you effectively integrate quotes, passages, and media to increase higher-level thinking?

Take Action

◆ Design an instructional task or assessment using a quote, passage, and/or media.

◆ Examine the instructional tasks and assessments you currently use. Where could you replace an instructional task or assessment with a quote, passage, and/or media to improve instructional quality?

Establishing a Culture of Thinking

Critical thinking must, therefore, command a place in any institution committed to the pursuit of education because critical thinking is a necessary condition of it.

—J.E. McPeck

To establish a culture of thinking in your classroom or school, teaching must transition from memorization to deeper applications of knowledge. Graphics, scenarios, and quotes provide a clear way of incorporating cognitively demanding instructional tasks and assessments. For many teachers, their K–12 experience did not include deep thinking experiences. To build a culture of thinking, teachers must embrace different instructional practices that nurture cognitive development.

Thinking is a skill that can be taught to all students. Teachers must intentionally plan cognitively demanding experiences in order for students to practice and develop their thinking capacities. When critical thinking is embedded in classroom instruction, students experience a rich array of opportunities that inherently develop their capacity to process information on higher levels. This chapter will discuss ways to establish a classroom culture that supports thinking and will recommend possible ways to incorporate interpretive exercises into formative and summative assessments.

Classroom Culture That Nurtures Thinking: Training the Brain

Classrooms can be work cultures or thinking cultures. Work cultures emphasize students completing assignments, but often at a low cognitive level. However, thinking cultures nurture students' thinking skills (Ritchhart, 2002). As Michael Michalko (2011) notes,

> We went to school. We were not taught how to think; we were taught to reproduce what past thinkers thought.... Instead of being taught to look for possibilities, we were taught to exclude them. It's as if we entered school as a question mark and graduated as a period. (p. 3)

Classrooms should encourage student questions and inquiries; student thinking should be the heart of the classroom.

There are several ways a teacher can purposefully enhance the enculturation of thinking: creating a physical environment promoting thinking, modeling the thinking process, teaching routines and structures for thinking, providing thinking opportunities, establishing clear expectations for thinking, and building supportive relationships to build thinking skills (Ritchhart, 2002). Just as people go to a gym to train their bodies to be stronger and more agile, teachers can train brains in a *thought-full* classroom.

Organize the Physical Environment

The physical environment of a gym can attract new customers. Some gyms post positive statements promoting fitness and strategically arrange the facility to better meet the needs of their customers. Similarly, the physical environment of the classroom can be organized to engage the brain. The visual cues and setup of the room can establish the importance of thinking. Posting high-level questions starters, as provided in the second chapter of this book, around the room prompts teachers and students to pose higher-level questions. Posters with engaging images and quotes can ignite student thinking. For example, the common quote, "Neurons that fire together wire together" can be an opening topic of conversation at the beginning of the school year. As students enter the room, the teacher can post a controversial question or quote for the current unit to immediately spark students' thinking about the content. For each unit, central questions such as "Is America progressing as a nation?" will challenge students to develop an overarching understanding of the lessons. The teacher can also list on the board lingering questions students have about the topics studied. This practice emphasizes that teachers do not have all the answers, but seek to deepen their understandings as well. Teachers can also designate a special lounge chair in the classroom for the "Socrates of the Day," celebrating a student who posed or answered a deep thinking question that day. Honoring good thinking should be a regular occurrence in thinking classrooms.

Establish the Importance of Critical Thinking Skills

When exercising, personal trainers and exercise instructors emphasize how a particular exercise benefits the body so their clients will understand the significance of the exercise. Likewise, at the beginning of the school year, students need to understand the reasons why critical thinking is important. The teacher can ask the class to generate a list of reasons why critical thinking would be imperative to their future success; students can then discuss the reasons why critical thinking is vital for personal and career success, as noted in the first chapter of this text. Just as teachers need to understand the reason for teaching thinking skills, students need to understand the positive effects of thinking. By establishing a focus on thinking, teachers can transform classrooms from mass-production classrooms with students able to answer fact-based questions to classrooms that embody real learning through thinking as students analyze, critique, and create.

Communicate Expectations for Thinking

When developing an exercise plan in the gym, clients identify their health goals. This establishes a target, whether it is to lose body fat or increase their level of activity. In the same way, students need clear thinking expectations. Grading criteria and models of student work should be shared with students. As students become more aware of their level of critical thinking, they should be encouraged to self-evaluate their performance based on the scoring guidelines. At the end of this chapter there is a critical-thinking rubric that can be used to assess the level of thinking on an assignment (see Take Action Figure 7.3 is on page 140). Before submitting their final product, students can self- and peer-assess their work based on the rubric, which teaches students to evaluate. In giving supportive and specific feedback during the peer-assessment, student reviewers can helpfully point out revisions to their partner's work and often realize changes to be made in their own work. When instructional tasks move from memorizing to thinking tasks, often a different type of student is more successful in your class—a deep thinker.

Establish Routines and Structures for Thinking

Some gyms help members design an exercise plan indicating the exact exercises that will be completed each week. Students need similar supports to organize their thinking. A thinking routine is a thinking strategy that has a few steps that are easy to teach and learn. This strategy can be used in a variety of contexts. Once a thinking routine is taught, it should be practiced frequently to develop competency. Several thinking routines and thinking structures are described along with the steps to implement the routine.

Numbered Heads

Students discuss questions in groups before the teacher asks questions. Students do not know whom the teacher will select so all students are prepared to answer.

1. The teacher divides students into groups and gives each group member a number.

2. The teacher poses a thoughtful question.

3. Groups discuss the answer.

4. The teacher calls a number and the person in each group with that number must respond to the question.

Think-Pair-Share

This routine gives students time to think individually before giving an answer, which is particularly helpful when higher-level thinking questions are posed (Lyman, 1981).

1. A question is posed.

2. Students individually think about the question and record their initial thoughts and/or answer.

3. Students share their thoughts with a partner.

4. Partners share their thoughts with the class.

Graphic Organizer/Concepts Map

Graphic organizers and concepts maps are another way for students to organize their thinking. Venn diagrams, flow charts, idea wheels, problem-solution charts, word webs, story maps, sequence charts, time lines, time-order charts, and persuasion maps are just some of the many types of organizers.

When teachers embed thinking routines into classroom instruction, students become active constructors of meaning. Learning begins with the students' thoughts as they develop their own initial ideas through the prompting of the questions in the thinking routines or the graphic organizer. These routines and the graphic organizers may be used in a group setting, which promotes sharing of diverse ideas and questions (Ritchhart, Palmer, Church, & Tishman, 2006). When teachers use certain routines or structures for thinking, they should use the name of the skill or routine to trigger the application—for instance, by saying "Evaluate ..." instead of "What are the positive aspects of...?" This encourages students to be familiar with the language.

Model Thinking Aloud

Many gyms provide staff to demonstrate to new members how to use the exercise equipment. Additionally, in exercise classes, teachers will model the appropriate way to complete the exercise. In classrooms, students need teachers to explain their thinking aloud so students become aware of the thinking processes involved in high-level thinking tasks. When interpretive exercises or high-level questions are first introduced, the teacher should model how to approach the question. Explicit modeling and making thinking visible to students has been shown to improve students' thinking processes (Ritchhart & Perkins, 2008). More direct approaches may be particularly important for struggling students. Students with few successful experiences thinking on higher levels will find teacher modeling particularly helpful as they see how expert thinkers reason. In addition, students can share their thinking processes with each other in groups to describe how they arrived at their conclusions or answers. Understanding others' thinking can help students reflect on their own thinking.

Provide Thinking Opportunities

To become physically fit, people must devote time to exercising. Just as in learning any new skill, with more time and opportunities, students will become more capable thinkers. If students are to become proficient thinkers, curriculum must focus on thinking, classrooms must be student-centered, developmentally appropriate practices must be followed, and students should learn to use their thinking skills in many different contexts.

Curriculum Focus on Thinking

In order to be better thinkers, students must have time to think. Schools must weed out some of the low-level curriculum, activities, and assessments thinking tasks that are not necessary and replace them with higher-level thinking tasks. Kurfiss (1988) states, "The characteristically American view that there is not 'time' to allow students to think has probably done considerable damage to learning" (p. 71). Schools need to build depth of understanding instead of focusing solely on covering a myriad of topics. Critical-thinking learning tasks require more instructional time but produce more lasting learning due to students having a deeper understanding after having completed them. It might mean selecting fewer concepts and teaching them to greater depths of understanding. So students see the broader concepts, teachers can structure lessons around themes: justice, change, power, patterns, conflict, forces, compromise, relationships, or passion.

Student-Centered Thinking

Thinking opportunities should be student-centered. Classroom discussions are a perfect opportunity for students to engage in debate if used correctly. Paul and Elder (2007) caution teachers, "Speak less so they can think more" (p. 44). Sometimes in classroom discussions teachers make most of the comments. Other times, the teacher poses deep thinking questions only to go ahead and answer the question aloud without giving students time to process their answer. In order to develop a critical manner, students should be encouraged to question each other. Teachers with thinking classrooms are willing to tolerate ambiguity and learn to suspend judgment as students develop their reasons. In a student-centered thinking classroom, the teacher is not seen as the source of all information or the determiner of the "correct answer." The teacher asks questions rather than telling information—a collaborative partnership in inquiry. Divergent opinions and thoughts are encouraged, and teachers should refrain from telling their own opinions lest they stifle the students' thinking processes.

Teachers can build lessons around questions, problems, and case studies to encourage active, experiential learning when students' natural curiosities are awakened. When students are deeply involved in a task and are willing to expend a large amount of effort to understand concepts or learn a skill, this is termed cognitive engagement (Boykin & Noguera, 2011). When teachers incorporate choices in the task and appeal to student's learning preferences, it increases the potential for cognitive engagement (Tishman, 2001). Thinking classrooms are full of challenge opportunities, student choice, and tasks that pique students' curiosity (Diamond & Hopson, 1999).

Developmentally Appropriate Practices

When designing thinking experiences, teachers should consider students' previous experiences and developmental levels. Posing a thought-provoking challenge allows teachers to assess the level of the students' thinking in order to establish a baseline of their current abilities. Baseline assessments can help teachers and students track the development of their critical thinking skills. In addition, baseline assessments give the teacher information on students' current abilities so as not to overestimate or underestimate students' skill levels. Based on students' current abilities, teachers can then set realistic expectations for students to develop their thinking skills. Tasks should provide an appropriate balance of challenge and support. If tasks are beyond the skill level of the students and the teacher does not give sufficient support, the students may become overwhelmed and produce poor work. Teachers may become disillusioned and revert to low-level thinking activities to improve the students' level of success. On the other hand, if tasks are not sufficiently challenging, students may lack motivation to create quality work. Teachers should select critical thinking tasks that challenge students to advance their abilities one step further. By scaffolding experiences to meet the individual needs of the student, teachers can help students gain a better sense of self-efficacy and become more motivated to tackle other thinking tasks (Lynch, Wolcott, & Huber, 2001). Gradually teachers should remove the scaffolds so students can independently complete thinking tasks.

Applying Thinking Skills in Multiple Contexts

Issues arise in the school and classroom that empower students to use thinking routines and devise a solution. For example, the class could work together and use the decision-making framework to solve a classroom management problem. Students often have difficulty applying thinking skills in contexts other than where they learned them. Using thinking skills to address classroom or school problems helps students learn to apply thinking routines and skills in many different contexts. Additionally, teachers can have students brainstorm a list of other situations where they could use the thinking skills practiced in the classroom in order to facilitate transfer of these abilities to different contexts.

Supportive Relationships and Interactions to Promote Thinking

To help a gym's clients reach their health goals, exercise instructors build positive relationships with the clients. With established relationships, exercise instructors can offer positive and helpful feedback to continually nudge clients toward their goals. When teachers build supportive relationships that promote thinking, students will be more willing to try difficult tasks. Clearly a teacher's negative response to student questions would inhibit critical thinking (Buck, 2002). Teachers should celebrate when students obviously have engaged in sophisticated thought processes. This might be through a verbal reinforcement—"Wow, deep thinking!"—or through a nonverbal response like a fist bump or a pat on the shoulder. I remember when a student who struggled in my class did exceptionally well on an open-ended response assessment. I asked the student to stay after class for a moment and then told him we were going to the office. There I asked him to call his parents. After dialing, he anxiously handed me the phone, probably remembering his frequent calls to his parents about disciplinary infractions. I told his mom in front of him that he had done extraordinarily well on an assessment by citing specific examples to support each point. I told her that I was extremely proud of his effort and structured thinking. His mother was thrilled and the boy smiled from ear to ear. Who doesn't like to hear good things about themselves?

When teachers encourage students and provide growth-oriented feedback, it can advance student thinking (Dweck, 2006). Constructive feedback focused on the connection between a student's ability and positive outcomes

Figure 7.1   **Feedback to Promote Student Thinking**

Feedback to Promote Student Thinking
◆ Affirm student's thinking. "Your ideas are important for us to hear."
◆ Ask for clarification. "Could you help me understand … ?"
◆ Request for elaboration. "Please tell us more about your thinking on this."
◆ Share feelings. "How did that make you feel?"
◆ Reflect on the thinking. "How did you come to that solution or conclusion?"
◆ Pursue reasoning. "What evidence supports your conclusions?"
◆ Inquire about opposing evidence. "What evidence doesn't support your conclusion or point of view?"
◆ Apply ideas. "How have you used this knowledge in other areas of your life?"
◆ Reflect. "What have you learned?"

Source: Costa, A. (Ed.). (2001). *Developing minds: A resource book for teaching thinking,* 3rd ed., pp. 108–109. Alexandria, VA: ASCD. © 2001 by ASCD. Reprinted with permission. Learn more about ASCD at www.ascd.org.

most likely will result in increased perceived self-efficacy and a tendency to seek out additional challenges (Bandura, 1997). Feedback should promote thinking by giving students specific ways they can improve their work (see Figure 7.1). If students think that their ideas will be rejected, they will be less likely to offer ideas. Teachers who respond negatively or allow other students to do so or cut off students when answering will reduce students' participation. Teachers should focus not on the right answer but on identifying how students arrived at the answer.

There are several identified conditions for establishing a thinking climate during class discussions. Teachers must listen carefully to students, showing respect for students and their ideas. When teachers and students listen and exchange ideas, the teacher-student relationship morphs into a partnership for learning, both learning from each other. By establishing a safe climate for ideas, teachers encourage students to pose questions and consider alternative viewpoints and ideas.

Another way to support students is through group work. Ritchhart & Perkins (2008) state that "the development of thinking is a social endeavor" (p. 58). Many of the thinking routines include opportunities to discuss with a partner or small group. Through the use of group work, students can engage in collaborative problem-solving and consider different perspectives. Group members can expose false assumptions and flawed thinking that someone individually might not recognize. Collaboration promotes conflict resolution, which requires thinking skills.

To encourage a thinking culture, students should be involved in decision-making processes in the organization of classrooms. For example, the class can design a plan to address the situation of peers inappropriately using the restrooms or working in groups. When teachers involve students in the decision-making of the classroom, it establishes a cooperative environment and gives students opportunities to apply their thinking skills to various contexts.

Finally, teachers should encourage students to learn from their mistakes and consider failure a part of the learning process. After failing, students should reflect on what went wrong and what they can do differently next time. Teachers should provide multiple opportunities for students to demonstrate their skills and understandings so students can improve their work.

Formatively Assessing Thinking

There are many ways to formatively assess thinking with engaging techniques. Marzano (2011) notes that if we "increase the number of students who respond we increase the chances of the information moving into working memory" (p. 12). To engage students in thinking about interpretive exercises, numerous strategies will be presented.

Strategies

Below is a list of some ways to formatively assess students' thinking.

- ◆ **Bell Ringer:** I strongly advocate that when students switch classes there should be a bell ringer on the board to engage students in content immediately. Bell ringers with interpretive exercises are a great way for a teacher to immediately engage students in the content as they enter the classroom. Bell ringers could review information from the day before or preassess students' knowledge of a topic.

- ◆ **Exit Ticket:** At the end of class, students respond to a question on a paper or index card to check their understanding of the lesson. The teacher can use the information to form differentiated groups the next day based on students' different levels of understanding.

- ◆ **Guess What?** At the beginning of class, a graphic, quote, or scenario is posed. Students then guess what they will be learning about that day.

- ◆ **Four Corners:** After students examine the introductory information in an interpretive exercise, a teacher poses a question and gives an A, B, C, or D answer choice. Students move to the corner designated for the answer choice they believe is the best answer. In the corners the group members discuss their answer. After a class discussion, the students can switch corners if they feel they need to change their answer.

- ◆ **Agree or Disagree:** As in Four Corners, the students examine the interpretive exercises and the teacher poses a controversial question. The room is divided in half and students stand on either side of the room depending on their answer. The class then engages in a debate about the question.

◆ **ABCD Cards:** Each student holds four cards, each printed with A, B, C, or D. The teacher poses a multiple-choice question and students answer by raising the appropriate card. Teachers can quickly collect formative assessment data on students' understanding of the content while giving students an opportunity to engage in a bodily-kinesthetic activity.

◆ **Classroom Response Systems:** Classroom response systems or clickers are a technological way to do the same thing as the ABCD cards. More sophisticated, this technology allows the teacher and/or class to view a data display showing how many students indicated each answer.

◆ **Computer or Cell Phone Polls:** For those who do not have a classroom response system, students can use computers or cell phones to answer multiple choice or open-ended questions. Websites like Poll Daddy, Poll Everywhere, and Wiffiti provide free services for this activity.

◆ **True/False Cards:** Just as students use the ABCD cards, students can use cards labeled True or False. The teacher reads a statement and students raise their card to indicate if the statement is true or false. The teacher can then ask why the statement is false.

◆ **True/Not True/True with Modification/Unable to Determine:** More advanced learners can classify a statement into one of four categories: True, Not True, True with Modification, or Unable to Determine (Himmele & Himmele, 2009). After students indicate their answer, the class could discuss reasons for voting for each option. A variation is for groups to work together to classify statements and then share their thoughts with the class.

◆ **Dry-Erase Boards:** Students respond to interpretive exercises with short answers on individual dry-erase boards. A cheaper method is giving students a sheet protector with a dry-erase marker.

◆ **Online Thought Boards:** Teachers pose an interpretive question and students respond online through Internet sites such as Wall Wisher and Lino It. Answers can then be categorized by grouping ideas on the online board.

◆ **Question Cube:** Students make a cube using online patterns with question starters for each side, such as "What consequence might happen if ... ?" or "Can you compare ... ?" Working in groups, students roll the cube and make a question using the starter. The group then discusses the answer to that question.

◆ **Students Write the Questions:** Groups formulate questions to ask other groups. Groups then exchange questions and answer the questions they've been given. For each thoughtful question or response to a question, groups can move a token to the center of their desk. This can be a game to accumulate as many tokens as possible by asking or answering questions thoughtfully.

- ◆ **Questioning Starters:** Use the question starter guide in the second chapter of this book to help you ask higher-level questions. There are also iPad and iPhone applications, including *Stick Pick*, which can help you track the questioning in your class. This application prompts you with question starters and can help you differentiate your question starters to different abilities in the class.

- ◆ **Graffiti Wall:** Teachers post interpretive exercises around the room along with questions and blank chart paper. Students move individually or in groups to each interpretive exercise and record answers to the questions, post questions, or add thoughts. Students are expected to add new insights on the chart paper near each interpretive exercise. Individuals or groups can use different color markers to identify their contributions.

- ◆ **Mystery:** The teacher gives groups several introductory materials and asks students to make inferences about what is happening. For example, to learn about an author, the students might be given quotes by the author, pictures of the covers of the author's books, and a news article. From all of these sources, the groups determine the best conclusions that can be made about the author. Also, the teacher could provide various introductory materials and ask groups to select only three to use. This would challenge students to really think about which materials would provide the most information on the author.

- ◆ **Inductive Learning:** Inductive learning involves giving groups five to eight introductory materials and having them classify them into larger categories that the students have to determine. For instance, students could be given visuals, real-world examples, and quotes about the water cycle and then decide how to categorize these materials into larger groups.

Think Time

With higher-level items, it is important that students are given time to think. The traditional three- to five-second window for think time needs to be dramatically extended to provide time for students to process the information and determine an answer. In fact, a simple test I use to determine if the question is higher-level is to think about how long it would take me to formulate an answer. If I can do it quickly, it is probably a lower-level question.

To prevent the fastest hand in the class from answering all the questions, a teacher could randomly select students by instituting a No Hands Up rule. With No Hands Up, the teacher records the student's names on craft sticks or slips of paper. An easy way is to make a copy of the student roster, cut apart the names, and place them in an envelope. The teacher poses the question and selects a name from the envelope or sticks to determine who gets the question. Teachers can also use online or smartphone applications like *Stick Pick* to randomly select students. This method of selecting students for questions keeps all students engaged because they never know who will be called on to answer the question.. To encourage students to pose questions to each other, the teacher can randomly select another student to answer the question posed.

If a student is called on and does not know the answer, the teacher might offer hints or let the student get assistance from a friend. However, to ensure that the called-on student understands, the student should be asked to summarize what was mentioned or add on to the answer given.

Differentiating

Bloom's taxonomy works seamlessly with differentiation. The teacher can pose an assignment about a given topic and provide options at different levels of the taxonomy. For example, after discussing political platforms, students could either (a) choose the ideas out of either of the political parties' platforms to design a platform that represents their views (Analyze/Evaluate level), or (b) create a new political platform that represent ideas for a new political party (Create level). Both options show high expectations, but they are differentiated to challenge all learners. Scholastic rigor is for all, and learning is enhanced when there is an appropriate level of challenge offered to students.

Real-World Interests

Students will be more interested in engaging in thinking activities when they connect to students' real-life experiences and interests (Ritchhart & Perkins, 2008). Teachers should select graphics, scenarios, and quotes that will engage the class in issues, problems, and practical situations that are appealing. If you are unsure of your students' interests, ask them. Many students are interested in sports, music, and media. Almost any topic can be connected to lyrics of songs. Sports and media also can be integrated into many subject areas. I remember asking my students what Bobby Knight and a dictatorship have in common. For those who did not know him, I provided a short description of his career. Making classroom connections to a wide variety of students' passions allows students to link information in new ways while appealing to students' interests.

Along with interests, teachers should allow student choice. There may be two different tasks to choose between, or students may select any media to support their opinion. Any time students are given a choice, they tend to be more motivated to complete the task.

Summative Assessments

The use of interpretive exercises in summative assessments can be included in a variety of formats. Teachers can use the exercises to prompt students' thinking. Students would then develop various products which demonstrate students' ability to Analyze, Evaluate, and Create, the top three levels of Bloom's revised taxonomy (Anderson & Krathwohl, 2001). Interpretive exercises can also be used in more traditional formats like multiple-choice assessments or open-ended writing tasks.

Students can use their understanding of interpretive exercises to design a variety of products, such as web pages, songs, museum exhibits, landscape designs, or new recipes. Often, assignments that produce a product work well with authentic tasks.

Critical-thinking skills can also be assessed in traditional formats, including multiple-choice and open-ended writing tasks. On a test, an interpretive exercise could include multiple questions to be answered based on one interpretive item. When used in this manner, often each subsequent question addresses a higher level of complexity. Below are some ways that interpretive exercises can be integrated into assessments in a multiple-choice format.

- ◆ Conclusion Follows/Conclusion Does Not Follow: After presenting interpretative materials a conclusion is stated with three multiple choice options: (a) the conclusion follows; (b) the conclusion does not follow; or (c) the conclusion is partially supported by the evidence.

  - ◇ Example: Based on the chart provided, more females than males failed the test.
    - a. The conclusion follows.
    - b. The conclusion does not follow.
    - c. The conclusion is partially supported by the evidence.

- ◆ Generalization: A generalization is reasoning from detailed facts to general principles. Students are asked to make a generalization or determine which generalization can be made from an interpretive exercise. Students select "S" if the statement is supported by the data in the table, "R" if the statement is refuted by the data in the table, or "N" if the statement is neither supported nor refuted by the data (Gronlund, 2006, p. 104).

  - ◇ Example: Based on the passage provided, bullying at the high school caused several suicides. Circle the correct answer: S, R, N

- ◆ Support/Oppose: After reviewing interpretive information, students are asked to choose if provided statements support or oppose the author's hypothesis.

- **Relevant Arguments:** After reading a passage, quote, scenario, or real-world example or listening to a media clip, students classify arguments posed as either relevant or irrelevant.

Interpretive exercises can also be used with essay and open-ended assessments, as shown in the examples in this text. With the four options above, students can choose the correct answer and then justify their answer in writing.

Summary

Building a culture of thinking in a classroom takes an intentional effort. A classroom culture that nurtures high cognitive demand includes a physical environment that promotes thinking, a clear priority to improve critical-thinking skills, developed routines and structures for thinking, teacher modeling of appropriate thinking practices, multiple and well-suited thinking opportunities, communicated expectations for thinking, and supportive relationships and interactions to promote thinking. When teachers use formative assessments with interpretive exercises to measure students' thinking abilities, they should utilize multiple formative assessment strategies, provide sufficient thinking time, differentiate, and connect to students' real-world interests. Summative assessments with interpretive exercises can be project-oriented, open-ended, or include forced-choice assessments like multiple-choice questions.

Discuss

1. How do you currently support a thinking culture in your school or classroom?

2. What are some ways to enhance the thinking culture in your school or classroom?

3. What metaphor would characterize a thinking classroom?

Take Action

1. Evaluate the level of thinking in your classroom by using the rating scale below (Figure 7.2). Circle the items on the table that are in your classroom or a part of your classroom practices.

2. Review the thinking routines in this chapter. Select one and implement it in your classroom.

3. A critical thinking rubric (Figure 7.3 on page 140) is included at the end of this chapter. When can you use this rubric to assess your students' critical thinking?

Figure 7.2 **Elements of a Classroom Culture That Nurtures Thinking**

Rating	Elements of a Classroom Culture That Nurtures Thinking
	Physical Environment ✓ Visual cues (e.g., posters, questions posted on the wall) promote thinking ✓ Organization of the room promotes thinking
	Establish the Importance of Critical Thinking Skills ✓ Early in the school year, students can clearly state the reasons for critical thinking
	Communicate Expectations for Thinking ✓ Grading criteria for thinking tasks are explained to students ✓ Models of student work are shared with students ✓ Students self-evaluate their work based on thinking criteria ✓ Peer assessment is used with thinking tasks
	Routines and Structures for Thinking ✓ Thinking routines are taught and regularly practiced
	Teacher Modeling ✓ Teacher models thinking
	Thinking opportunities ✓ Students are given many opportunities to refine their thinking abilities ✓ Curriculum focuses on deep understandings ✓ Students question each other ✓ Divergent opinions and thoughts are encouraged ✓ Thinking tasks appeal to students' learning preferences and curiosity and provide student choice ✓ Pre-assessments measure students' abilities in order to determine appropriate tasks ✓ Students apply thinking skills in multiple contexts
	Supportive Relationships and Interactions to Promote Thinking ✓ Student questions are encouraged ✓ Teacher provides appropriate feedback ✓ Students are engaged in collaborative tasks ✓ Students are involved in the classroom decision-making process ✓ Teacher supports learning from mistakes

Figure 7.3 **Holistic Scoring Guide**

The Holistic Critical Thinking Scoring Rubric A Tool for Developing and Evaluating Critical Thinking
Strong 4—Consistently does all or almost all of the following: ◆ Accurately interprets evidence, statements, graphics, questions, etc. ◆ Identifies the most important arguments (reasons and claims) pro and con. ◆ Thoughtfully analyzes and evaluates major alternative points of view. ◆ Draws warranted, judicious, non-fallacious conclusions. ◆ Justifies key results and procedures, explains assumptions and reasons. ◆ Fair-mindedly follows where evidence and reasons lead.
Acceptable 3—Does most or many of the following: ◆ Accurately interprets evidence, statements, graphics, questions, etc. ◆ Identifies relevant arguments (reasons and claims) pro and con. ◆ Offers analyses and evaluations of obvious alternative points of view. ◆ Draws warranted, non-fallacious conclusions. ◆ Justifies some results or procedures, explains reasons. ◆ Fair-mindedly follows where evidence and reasons lead.
Unacceptable 2—Does most or many of the following: ◆ Misinterprets evidence, statements, graphics, questions, etc. ◆ Fails to identify strong, relevant counter-arguments. ◆ Ignores or superficially evaluates obvious alternative points of view. ◆ Draws unwarranted or fallacious conclusions. ◆ Justifies few results or procedures, seldom explains reasons. ◆ Regardless of the evidence or reasons, maintains or defends views based on self-interest or preconceptions.
Weak 1—Consistently does all or almost all of the following: ◆ Offers biased interpretations of evidence, statements, graphics, questions, information, or the points of view of others. ◆ Fails to identify or hastily dismisses strong, relevant counter-arguments. ◆ Ignores or superficially evaluates obvious alternative points of view. ◆ Argues using fallacious or irrelevant reasons, and unwarranted claims. ◆ Does not justify results or procedures, nor explain reasons. ◆ Regardless of the evidence or reasons, maintains or defends views based on self-interest or preconceptions. ◆ Exhibits close-mindedness or hostility to reason.

Source: From P. Facione & N.C. Facione. (1994). *Holistic critical thinking scoring rubric.*
Reprinted with permission of California Academic Press.

Conclusion

Some people study all their life and at their death they have learned everything except to THINK.
—François-Urbain Domergue

It is 2:30 p.m. on the last day of school, and the buses will roll out of the parking lot at 3 p.m. The school counselor announces that money has been stolen from her purse—$300 in cash. Is the culprit a student or a staff member? With no previous instances of stealing in the front office, it seems improbable that this is a staff issue. Teachers and other staff were attending the awards ceremony in the gym, leaving few people in the office. A secretary comments that she had caught a student at 11 a.m. looking around my office, the principal's office, and told him to go back to class. After considering the possible hypotheses, we agree that a student roaming in the front office while administrators were at an awards ceremony seems a likely suspect. Another office worker mentions that she had observed the same student in the counselor's office at 11:30 a.m. and told him to go to class. With two accounts from two reliable witnesses, the evidence seems to point toward the roaming student. Staff members find him in class—it is 2:45 p.m. He denies the charge and his belongings are searched. No evidence of the money is found.

It is five minutes until the buses arrive. The choices are to send the student home on the bus or retain him for further questioning. A decision is made, based on two credible eyewitness testimonies of suspicious behavior in the front office, that the student should be detained. When a teacher, a school counselor, and the principal try to extract the truth, the student again denies the charge. Parents and then police are called. The parent warns the student to tell the truth to the police officer. After a one-hour discussion with the police officer, the student admits that he stole the money and reveals its hiding place—between the cushions in the front-office couch.

With thirty minutes left on the clock on our last day, I had to make a quick, thoughtful decision in this situation. First, I had to understand the situation by gathering information from all sources. In this case, a student was going to be investigated, and I needed to consider whether the information was from a reliable source. Ultimately, by 2:45, I had to make a decision whether there was sufficient evidence to continue questioning him or whether I should let him go home on the bus, knowing that, since this was the last school day of the year, it would be difficult to talk to him again and if he had stolen the money it would probably never be recovered.

This is real life—convoluted and complicated. Our students, currently and in their future careers and life situations, encounter similar problematic issues. We as educators have the power to equip them with skills to handle these situations thoughtfully and make good decisions. The job will necessitate letting go of some tasks and assessments that require little thinking, while challenging students to be 21st-century learners as they wade into the complex issues of the content areas you teach. Henry Ford said, "Thinking is hard work, and that's why so few people do it."

Through this text I have tried to make a case for the importance of critical thinking. Misconceptions regarding thinking were addressed, and a detailed description of Bloom's revised taxonomy was provided. To help educators design higher-level thinking tasks and assessments, interpretive exercises were presented as one way to meet that need. Scenarios, real-world examples, and authentic tasks provide a method to assess students in a close to real-world context. Visuals, including illustrations, maps, diagrams, data tables, and charts, appeal to visual learners while also engaging them in higher-level thinking. Short quotes, passages, and media clips are another approach to challenge students to understand, analyze, and evaluate information. Finally, the text showcased ways to build a thinking culture in a classroom along with formative and summative assessment ideas.

The intention of this text is to enhance teachers' understanding of high-level thinking tasks and assessments. Now it is time for action. The first step is for teachers to assess the level of thinking in their classroom and select several ideas in this text that they can apply immediately. An Implementation Chart (Figure 8.1) is included at the end of this chapter to help teachers make a plan.

Thinking skills will equip students for college, work, and daily life. By building a classroom culture that supports thinking, teachers can prime their students for all these experiences. Thanks to these efforts, students will be prepared to meet the challenges and changes in our century with success.

Discuss

1. What are three ideas in the text you can immediately implement?

2. What statements in the text have been most helpful in improving your professional practices?

Take Action

1. Complete the Implementation Chart (Figure 8.1). Indicate your specific goals, how you will measure them, and the time frame for completing them.

2. Identify another teacher, perhaps one who is in a professional learning community with you. Share your implementation goals, and agree on a date when you will meet to consider evidence of completing the goals. After you have implemented your goals, meet with your colleague and consider evidence of how you executed your plan. Discuss successes, ways to improve, and next steps you can take to continue enhancing the thinking skills in your classroom.

Figure 8.1 **Implementation Chart**

Specific Goal	Measure	Time Frame
Example: *I will include visual interpretive exercises at the beginning of class (bell ringers) to improve my students' higher-level thinking skills.*	*I will assess student performance on these items weekly.*	*I will do this daily during the first quarter of the semester.*

References

Achieve. (2006). *Closing the expectations gap 2006: An annual 50-state progress report on the alignment of high school policies with the demands of college and work.* Retrieved from www.achieve.org/files/50-state-06-Final.pdf.

ACT. (2006). *Ready to succeed: All students prepared for college and work.* Retrieved from www.act.org/research/policymakers/pdf/ready_to_succeed.pdf.

ACT. (2011). *The condition of college and career readiness 2011.* Retrieved from www.act.org/readiness/2011.

Anderson, L.W., & Krathwohl, D.R. (Eds.). (2001). *A taxonomy for learning, teaching, and assessing: A revision of Bloom's Taxonomy of Educational Objectives* (complete edition). New York: Longman.

Bandura, A. (1997). *Self-efficacy: The exercise of control.* New York: W.H. Freeman.

Blackburn, B. R. (2008). *Rigor is not a four-letter word.* New York: Eye On Education.

Bloom, B. S. (Ed.). (1956). *Taxonomy of educational objectives: The classification of educational goals, by a committee of college and university examiners. Handbook I: Cognitive domain.* New York: David McKay.

Boykin, A. W., & Noguera, P. (2011). *Creating the opportunity to learn: Moving from research to practice to close the achievement gap.* Alexandria, VA: ASCD.

Bradley, P. (2012). *Introduction to fake websites.* Retrieved from www.philb.com/fakesites.htm.

Browne, M. L., & Keeley, S. M. (2004). *Asking the right questions: A guide to critical thinking* (7th ed.). Upper Saddle River, NJ: Pearson Education.

Buck, G. A. (2002). Teaching discourses: Science teachers' responses to the voices of adolescent girls. *Learning Environments Research, 5,* 29–50.

Chaffee, J. (1988). *Thinking critically.* Boston: Houghton Mifflin.

Chaffee, J. (2006). *Thinking critically* (8th ed.). Wilmington, MA: Wadsworth.

Chartrand, J., Ishikawa, H., & Flander, S. (2009). *Critical thinking means business: Learn to apply and develop the new #1 workplace skill.* Upper Saddle River, NJ: Pearson Education. Retrieved from www.talentlens.com/en/downloads/whitepapers/Pearson_TalentLens_Critical_Thinking_Means_Business.pdf.

Civic Enterprises. (2006). *The silent epidemic: Perspectives of high school dropouts.* Washington, DC: Civic Enterprises. Retrieved from www.gatesfoundation.org/ unitedstates/Documents/TheSilentEpidemic3-06FINAL.pdf.

The Conference Board, Inc., The Partnership for 21st Century Skills, Corporate Voices for Working Families, and Society for Human Resource Management. (2006). *Are they really ready to work? Employers' perspectives on the basic knowledge and applied skills of new entrants to the 21st century U.S. workforce.* New York: The Conference Board.

Costa, A. (Ed.). (2001). *Developing minds: A resource book for teaching thinking,* 3rd ed., pp. 108–109. Alexandria, VA: ASCD.

Day, M., Stobaugh, R., & Tassell, J. L. (2010, December). *Boosting the cognitive complexity of science assessments.* Presentation at the annual meeting of National Science Teachers Association Area Conference on Science Education, Nashville, TN.

Diamond, M., & Hopson, J. (1999). *Magic trees of the mind: How to nurture your child's intelligence, creativity, and healthy emotions form birth through adolescence.* New York: Penguin/Plume.

Dweck, C. (2006). *Mindset: The new psychology of success.* New York: Ballantine.

Facione, P. A. (1990a). *Technical report #1: Experimental validity and content validity.* Millbrae: California Academic Press. (ERIC 327 549).

Facione, P. A. (1990b). *Technical report #2: Factors predictive of CT skills.* East Lansing, MI: National Center for Research on Teacher Learning. (ERIC ED 327 550).

Facione, P. A. (2011). *Think critically.* Englewood Cliffs, NJ: Pearson Education.

Facione, P. A., Facione, N. C., & Giancarlo, C. F. (1992). *The California critical thinking disposition inventory: Test manual.* Millbrae: California Academic Press.

Fleming, M., & Chambers, B. (1983). Teacher-made tests: Windows on the classroom. In W. E. Hathaway (Ed.), *Testing in the schools* (pp. 29–38). San Francisco: Jossey-Bass

Fogarty, R. (1997). *Brain compatible classrooms.* Arlington Heights, IL: Skylight Training.

Frisby, C. L. (1992). Construct validity and psychometric properties of the Cornell critical thinking test (Level Z): A contrasted group analysis. *Psychological Reports, 71,* 291–303.

Gabel, D., & National Science Teachers Association. (1994). *Handbook of research on science teaching and learning.* New York: Macmillan

Goodlad, J. I. (2004). *A place called school* (2nd ed.). New York: McGraw-Hill.

Gronlund, N. E. (1981). *Measurement and evaluation in teaching.* New York: Macmillan.

Gronlund, N. E. (2006). *Assessment of student achievement* (8th ed.). Boston: Pearson Education.

Haladyna, T. M., Downing, S. M., & Rodriguez, M. C. (2002). A review of multiple-choice item-writing guidelines for classroom assessment. *Applied Measurement in Education, 15* (3), 309–334. doi: 10.1207/S15324818AME1503_5.

Hale, C. D., & Astolfi, D. M. (2011). *Measuring learning and performance: A primer* (2nd ed.). Retrieved from www.CharlesDennisHale.com.

Himmele, P., & Himmele, W. (2009). *The language-rich classroom: A research based framework for teaching English language learners.* Alexandria, VA: ASCD.

Insight Assessment. (n.d.). *Characteristics of critical thinking.* Retrieved from www.insightassessment.com/.

Jacobs, S. S. (1995). Technical characteristics and some correlates of the California Critical Thinking Skills Test forms A and B. *Higher Education Research, 36,* 89–108.

Kentucky Department of Education. (2011). *Sample content for the Kentucky state assessment from the Stanford Achievement Test series.* Retrieved from www.education.ky.gov/KDE/Administrative+Resources/Testing+ and+Reporting+/District+Support/Link+to+Released+Items/Sample+ Assessment+Items+for+K-PREP.htm.

King, P. M., Wood, P. K., & Mines, R. A. (1990). Critical thinking among college and graduate students. *Review of Higher Education, 13* (2), 167–186.

Klaczynski, P. A. (2001). Analytic and heuristic processing influences on adolescent reasoning and decision making. *Child Development, 72,* 844–861.

Kurfiss, J. G. (1988). *Critical thinking: Theory, research, practice and possibilities. ASHE-ERIC Higher Education Report No. 2.* Washington, DC: Association for the Study of Higher Education.

Lemke, M., Sen, A., Pahlke, E., Partelow, L., Miller, D., Williams, T., Kastberg, D., & Jocelyn, L. (2004). *International outcomes of learning in mathematics literacy and problem solving: PISA 2003. Results from the U.S. perspective.* (NCES 2005–003). Washington, DC: U.S. Department of Education, National Center for Education Statistics.

Lyman, F. T. (1981). The responsive classroom discussion: The inclusion of all students. In A. Anderson (Ed.), *Mainstreaming digest* (pp. 109–113). College Park: University of Maryland Press.

Lynch, C. L., Wolcott, S. K., & Huber, G. E. (2001). *Steps for better thinking: A developmental problem solving process.* Retrieved from www.WolcottLynch.com.

Madaus, G. F., West, M. M., Harmon, M. C., Lomax, R. G., & Viator, K. A. (1992). *The influence of testing on teaching math and science in grades 4–12: Executive summary.* Chestnut Hill, MA: Boston College, Center for the Study of Testing, Evaluation, and Educational Policy.

Marzano, R. J. (2011). *The highly engaged classroom.* Bloomington, IN: Marzano Research Laboratories.

Marzano, R. J., Pickering, D. J., & Pollock, J. E. (2001). *Classroom instruction that works: Research-based strategies for increasing student achievement.* Alexandria, VA: ASCD.

Maxwell, M., Stobaugh, R., & Tassell, J. (2012). *CReaTe Framework.* Unpublished manuscript.

Mayer, R. E. (1999). *The promise of educational psychology: Learning in the content areas.* Upper Saddle River, NJ: Prentice Hall.

Mayer, R. E., & Wittrock, M. S. (1996). Problem-solving transfer. In D. C. Berliner and R. C. Calfee (Eds.), *Handbook of educational psychology* (pp. 47–62). New York: Macmillan.

Mehrens, W. A., & Lehmann, I. J. (1984). *Measurement and evaluation in education and psychology* (3rd ed.). New York: Holt, Rinehart & Winston.

MetLife. (2011). *The MetLife survey of the American teacher: Preparing students for college and careers.* Retrieved from www.metlife.com/about/corporate-profile/citizenship/metlife-foundation/metlife-survey-of-the-american-teacher.html?WT.mc_id=vu1101.

Michalko, M. (2011). *Creative thinkering.* Novato, CA: New World Library.

Mines, R. A., King, P. M., Hood, A. B., & Wood, P. K. (1990). Stages of intellectual development and associated critical thinking skills in college students. *Journal of College Student Development, 31,* 538–547.

Moore, B., & Stanley, T. (2010). *Critical thinking and formative assessments: Increasing the rigor in your classroom.* Larchmont, NY: Eye On Education.

National Center for Education Statistics. (2011). *The condition of education 2011.* Retrieved from http://nces.ed.gov/pubs2011/2011033_4.pdf.

National Center on Education and the Economy. (2008). *Tough choices or tough times: The report of the New Commission on the Skills of the American Workforce.* Washington, DC: National Center on Education and the Economy.

National Governors Association Center for Best Practices, Council of Chief State School Officers. (2010a). *Common core state standards for English language arts & literacy in history/social studies, science, and technical subjects.* Washington, DC: Author. Retrieved from www.corestandards.org/assets/CCSSI_ELA%20Standards.pdf.

National Governors Association Center for Best Practices, Council of Chief State School Officers. (2010b). *Common core state standards for math.* Washington, DC: Author. Retrieved from www.corestandards.org/assets/CCSSI_Math%20Standards.pdf.

Nitko, A. J. (1983). *Educational tests and measurement: An introduction.* New York: Harcourt Brace Jovanovich.

Nitko, A. J., & Brookhart, S. M. (2007). *Educational assessment of students* (5th ed.). Upper Saddle River, NJ: Pearson Education.

Olson, K. (2009). *Wounded by school.* New York: Teachers College Press.

The Partnership for 21st Century Skills (2011). *P21 Common Core Toolkit: A Guide to Aligning the Common Core State Standards with the Framework for 21st Century Skills.* Washington, DC: The Partnership for 21st Century Skills.

Paul, R., & Elder, L. (2005). *A guide for educators to critical thinking competency standards.* Dillon Beach, CA: Foundation for Critical Thinking.

Paul, R., & Elder, L. (2007). *A guide for educators to critical thinking competency standards* (2nd ed.). Dillon Beach, CA: Foundation for Critical Thinking.

Paul, R., & Nosich, G. M. (1992). *A model for the national assessment of higher order thinking.* Santa Rosa, CA: Foundation for Critical Thinking.

Perkins, D. N. (1995). *Outsmarting IQ: The emerging science of learnable intelligence.* New York: Free Press.

Pogrow, S. (1990). Challenging at-risk learners: Finds from the HOTS program. *Phi Delta Kappan, 71* (5), 389–397.

Pogrow, S. (1994). Helping learners who "just don't understand." *Educational Leadership, 52* (3), 62–66.

Raths, J. (2002). Improving instruction. *Theory into Practice, 41* (4), 233–237.

Raudenbush, S. W., Rowan, B., & Cheong, Y. F. (1993). The pursuit of higher-order instructional goals in secondary schools: Class, teacher, and school influences. *American Educational Research Journal, 30*, 523–553.

Ray, B. (2012). *Design thinking: Lessons for the classroom.* Retrieved from www.edutopia.org/blog/design-thinking-betty-ray.

Reed, S. K. (2000). Problem solving. In A. E. Kazdin (Ed.), *Encyclopedia of psychology* (8th ed.), pp. 71–75. Washington, DC: American Psychological Association.

Reich, R. (1989). *The resurgent liberal: And other unfashionable prophecies.* New York: Random House.

Ritchhart, R. (2002). *Intellectual character: What it is, why it matters and how to get it.* San Francisco: Jossey-Bass.

Ritchhart, R., Palmer, P., Church, M., & Tishman, S. (2006). *Thinking routines: Establishing patterns of thinking in the classroom.* Retrieved from www.pz.harvard.edu/research/AERA06Thinking Routines.pdf.

Ritchhart, R., & Perkins, D. (2008). Making thinking visible. *Educational Leadership, 65* (5), 57–61.

Rotherham, A. J., & Willingham, D. (2009). 21st century skills: The challenges ahead. *Educational Leadership, 67* (1), 16–21.

Schamel, D., & Ayres, M. P. (1992). The minds-on approach: Student creativity and personal involvement in undergraduate science laboratory. *Journal of College Science Teaching 21*, 226–229.

Shepard, L. (2001). The role of classroom assessment in teaching and learning. In V. Richardson (Ed.), *Handbook of research on teaching* (4th ed.) (pp. 1066–1101). Washington, DC: American Educational Research Association.

Shepard, L., Hammerness, K., Darling-Hammond, L., & Rust, F. (2005). Assessment. In L. Darling-Hammond & J. Bransford (Eds.), *Preparing teachers for a changing world: What teachers should learn and be able to do* (pp. 275–326). San Francisco: Jossey-Bass.

Siegler, R. S. (1998). *Children's thinking* (3rd ed.). Upper Saddle River, NJ: Prentice-Hall.

Silva, E. (2008). *Measuring skills for the 21st century.* Washington, DC: Education Sector Reports.

Stanley, S. (2006). *Creating an enquiring mind.* London: Continuum International.

Sternberg, R. J. (2008). *Cognitive psychology* (5th ed.). Belmont, CA: Thomson-Wadsworth.

Stiggins, R. J., Arter, J. A., Chappuis, J., & Chappuis, S. (2004). *Classroom assessment for student learning: Doing it right—using it well.* Portland, OR: Assessment Training Institute.

Stobaugh, R., Day, M. M., Tassell, J. L., & Blankenship, H. (2011). Boosting cognitive complexity in social studies assessments. *Social Studies and the Young Learner, 23*, 4–8.

Suskie, L. (2009). *Assessing student learning: A common sense guide* (2nd ed.). San Francisco: Jossey-Bass.

Swartz, R. J., & Parks, S. (1994). *Infusing critical and creative thinking into content instruction: A lesson design handbook for elementary grades.* Pacific Grove, CA: Critical Thinking Press and Software.

3M Corporation. (2001). *Polishing your presentation.* 3M Meeting Network Articles & Advice.

Tishman, S. (2001). Added value: A dispositional perspective on thinking. In A. L. Costa (Ed.), *Developing minds: A resource book for teaching thinking* (pp. 72–75). Alexandria, VA: ASCD.

Tomlinson, C. A., & Javius, E. L. (2012). Teach up for excellence. *Educational Leadership, 69* (5), 28–33.

Torff, B. (2005). Developmental changes in teachers' beliefs about critical-thinking activities. *Journal of Educational Psychology, 92,* 13–22.

Torff, B. (2006). Expert teachers' beliefs about critical-thinking activities. *Teacher Education Quarterly, 33,* 37–52.

Torff, B. (2008). Using the critical thinking belief appraisal to assess the rigor gap. *Learning Inquiry, 2,* 29–52.

Torff, B. (2011). Teacher beliefs shape learning for all students. *Phi Delta Kappan, 93* (3), 21–23.

Torres, R. M. (1993). *The cognitive ability and learning style of students enrolled in the College of Agriculture at The Ohio State University.* Unpublished doctoral dissertation. Columbus: Ohio State University

U.S. Department of Education, Office of Planning, Evaluation and Policy Development. (2010). *A blueprint for reform: The reauthorization of the Elementary and Secondary Education Act.* Washington, DC: Author.

Vosniadou, S. (2001). How children learn: Educational practices, series 7. *International Academy of Education.* Geneva, Switzerland: International Bureau of Education. Retrieved from www.ibe.unesco.org/fileadmin/user_upload/archive/publications/EducationalPracticesSeriesPdf/prac07e.pdf.

Wainer, H., & Kiely, G. (1987). Item clusters and computerized adaptive testing: A case for testlets. *Journal of Educational Measurement, 24,* 185–202.

Wenglinsky, H. (2000). *How teaching matters: Bringing the classroom back into discussion of teacher quality.* Princeton, NJ: Educational Testing Service.

Wenglinsky, H. (2002). The link between teacher classroom practices and student academic performance. *Education Policy Analysis Archives, 10,* 12. Retrieved from http://epaa.asu.edu/ojs/article/view/291.

Wenglinsky, H. (2003). Using large-scale research to gauge the impact of instructional practices on student reading comprehension: An exploratory study. *Education Policy Analysis Archives, 11,* 19. Retrieved from http://epaa.asu.edu/ojs/article/view/247.

Zohar, A., & Dori, J. (2003). Higher-order thinking and low-achieving students: Are they mutually exclusive? *Journal of the Learning Sciences, 12,* 145–182.